SHOGUN'S
GHOST

SHOGUN'S GHOST
THE DARK SIDE OF JAPANESE EDUCATION

KEN SCHOOLLAND

BERGIN & GARVEY
New York • Westport, Connecticut • London

378.52
S

Library of Congress Cataloging-in-Publication Data

Schoolland, Ken.
    Shogun's ghost : the dark side of Japanese education / Ken
Schoolland.
        p.   cm.
    Includes bibliographical references (p.).
    ISBN 0-89789-218-6 (lib. bdg. : alk. paper)
    1. Education—Social aspects—Japan   2. School discipline—Japan.
3. Corporal punishment—Japan   4. School violence—Japan.
5. Education—Japan—Evaluation.   I. Title.
LC191.8.J3S36   1990
378.52—dc20   90-32124

Library of Congress Catalog Card Number: 90-32124
ISBN: 0-89789-218-6

First published in 1990

Bergin & Garvey, One Madison Avenue, New York, NY 10010
An imprint of Greenwood Publishing Group, Inc.

Printed in the United States of America

The paper used in this book complies with the
Permanent Paper Standard issued by the National
Information Standards Organization (Z39.48-1984).

10 9 8 7 6 5 4 3 2

Copyright Acknowledgments

Grateful acknowledgment is given to the editors of the *Asahi Evening News* and the
Mainichi Daily News for permission to reprint letters to the editor, as well as editori-
als. "Runaway," music by Tadao Inoue, lyrics by Reiko Yukawa, © 1980 by
Fujipacific Music Inc. Used by permission of JASRAC (Japanese Society for Rights
of Authors, Composers, and Publishers), License No. 9070095.

For their inspiration and for their contributions on behalf of youth rights, this book is dedicated to:

Hirofumi Shikagawa
Kazu Tomisawa
Toshio Murata
Hitoshi Maruyama
Yoshio Murakami
Takahashi Hayashi
Minoru Yamamoto
Ko Mori
& Bob Krel

CONTENTS

PREFACE

Hakodate is the most beautiful town in Hokkaido, the forested, northernmost island of Japan. The main industries are fishing and shipbuilding, both in decline, and tourism and education, which seem to be doing well. Slightly off the beaten track for most travelers to Japan, this is a town that is frequented by very few foreigners despite its rather sizable population of 330,000. This was not always so.

Hakodate was one of the first three ports to be opened to trade with the West following the visit of Commodore Matthew Perry in the 1850s. Nevertheless, contact with the outside world peaked very early, and ships have largely bypassed Hakodate since World War II. When I arrived in 1984, there seemed to be fewer than a dozen Westerners in the entire city.

This was an exciting adventure for me, and I looked forward to teaching my first classes in a Japanese university. Hawaii Loa College had an exchange program with Hakodate University, my sponsor, and I wound up teaching at two other colleges in Japan as well.

It seemed as if most of the staff and faculty from our sister school greeted me at the airport when I arrived that August afternoon. They treated me like royalty, introducing me to the press and local dignitaries, and invited me to welcoming parties and a picnic in my honor.

The university provided me with generous assistance in obtaining virtually every necessity for comfortable living. They offered me a subsidized apartment at ¥5,000 a month ($20 in 1984), which included all utilities and appliances (usually an extra expense in Japan), a third of my annual income in bonuses (which increased rapidly in value relative to the dollar), plenty of travel allowances, and even a $400 shortwave radio so that I could keep up with foreign news. I soon made friends among the faculty who helped me with every major and minor problem that popped up.

Even on campus I was provided with an office many times more spacious than anything I had had in my teaching career. The secretarial services and amenities of the post were remarkably generous. And I was impressed with the scholarly competence of the faculty. This was certainly teacher's heaven.

Back Door Escape

This heavenly bliss was quickly shaken on my first day of classes. I walked into a room that was packed with students, all sitting behind long rows of wooden desks that were fastened to the floor.

The room could hold one-hundred students, and my class of fifty was plastered to the desks farthest from the front. It was almost comical. As I walked past other classrooms, it was not at all unusual to see a professor lecturing to six or seven students—all of whom lined the back rows as if the professor suffered a terrible case of halitosis.

It was no easy task to teach to a group that size, not if you had been accustomed to small colleges in Alaska and Hawaii with a maximum of 30 students in rooms that were always fairly cozy. This university was relatively small, with just over 800 students total, yet first-year classes were enormous. And at the national universities, first-year English classes could be much larger yet. I feel a lingering twinge of sympathy for the poor teacher who followed me at Hakodate University. He claims that his English classes now reach upwards of one-hundred students.

But it was not the size of the class that was disturbing. It was the atmosphere. In all my previous years of college teaching I had never experienced any serious disciplinary problems. No chronic talking or sleeping during class. No mass exodus when my back was turned. No widespread cheating or disruption. That is one reason why I chose to teach at the college level. Students always seemed fairly capable of behaving themselves. But in my new university post in Japan, I walked into pandemonium.

My predecessor tried to prepare me for the job by warning me that the students here were completely different than anything I had ever experienced. These students, I was warned, were virtually impossible to control.

I didn't believe him. This was the opposite of all I had read and heard about Japan over years of study. But it was true. And peering into other classrooms or talking to other professors made me feel that this was not just a problem in my own classes.

These young people, almost all boys, half of them wearing what looked like black military uniforms, were the noisiest, most unruly pack I had ever experienced in my life. Before this, I had imagined that such a "blackboard jungle" only existed at junior high schools in the Bronx, especially when a substitute teacher walked into class for a day. By the end of the first week, I was almost ready to quit.

As soon as roll was taken, what little of it could be heard over the persistent clamor, nearly a dozen students "escaped" out the back door—and I wanted to go with them. Most of those who remained in their seats seemed to be absorbed in little games and laughter. Was this university education?

As time went on I was stunned to find cheating to be rampant. Tests were administered on one day to all the students taking a required course at a certain level. The students were seated in rows, carefully separated from each other by an empty seat, and they were monitored by two instructors who roamed the isles. Two monitors were required so that one could always watch the other. To no avail.

On one accounting examination it appeared that maybe ten of the fifty students were well prepared for the test while the rest simply slept or sat with a blank stare for most of the hour. As I looked over their shoulders, only fourteen of the students seemed to know anything about a relatively simple question on depreciation.

The youths playfully tried every blatant method of cheating, and they were often caught. The cheating was fairly crude, and little effort was made to disguise the intent. Usually students just nudged closer to each other, straining to get a glimpse at each other's exam. Frequently, students pulled out crib sheets. Some came into the room early so they could scribble volumes of notes onto a desk before the exam.

All of this was relatively safe activity because they were quite certain that nothing would be done about it. Catching a few, I thought I would make an example to the other students by turning them in to another regular teacher who was monitoring the exam with me. To my surprise, the other teacher just grinned and shrugged when I told him of the infractions. The penalty? "Tell them not to do it, and watch them more closely."

Polite Influence

Even after the final grades were handed out, there seemed to be extraordinary pressure from students, faculty, and parents not to fail anyone. When it was learned that I was going to fail a few students, a couple of teachers came to speak to me about those cases.

"Is there anything they could do to make up the final exam? Could they do some additional work?" asked one professor.

Still another professor said, "My good friend is the uncle of your student, and he has expressed serious concern over the possibility that his nephew might fail. What can be done to help him pass the test in your class?" Such were the questions even after the final exam.

Tests might be given over and over until all the students passed. After the third retake of an English test, it was at last agreed that one student should be required to do the year-long course over again because it was abundantly clear that little effort had been given to his studies. This student had only attended one class period during the entire semester.

At another time gifts were given by parents, presumably as "thank you money," but clearly intended to influence the professors. Tailor-made shirts, bottles of premium whiskey, and fine dining could all be part of the cultivation of a professor's favor toward a son or daughter.

I was later told that it is not uncommon for parents to give gifts to influence teachers in the lower grades as well. It is then hoped that the teachers would be encouraged to give good student reports.

Gifts to public university faculty were illegal, and gifts for low-level private colleges were probably unimportant. But the significance of gifts rose with the status of institutions.

"'Thank you money' is routine in many circumstances," explained the wife of a college professor one day. "A member of the faculty at a medical university might get as much as a million yen in 'thank you money' from a student. For a doctoral degree in the science divisions it might range from ¥30,000 to ¥50,000 ($230–$390)—more if the professor is a chairman of the review committee."

I was skeptical about all of this until I, too, had been discretely offered such "gifts." The audacity of it all convinced me that such things must be pretty widely accepted.

As political scandals unraveled on the national scene, I expected to find people to be upset about influence peddling at the top levels of government. Instead, it seemed that thank you money for favors was tolerated as a natural, polite part of doing politics or business, regardless of the endeavors.

The problem with fallen politicos, like Kakuei Tanaka and Noboru Takeshita, was that they had not been subtle enough to keep some embarrassing, up-start journalist from noticing. And the whole of Japanese society seemed to take more of a concerned interest in these matters when foreigners started to write articles.

Perhaps if I was looking at American culture with fresh eyes, it would be easier to recognize variations of this behavior that are just as widespread in the United States. Certainly Americans have grown quite complacent about myriad pay-offs to their own politicians. And Americans also perk up and take greater notice of problems when foreigners point the accusing finger.

A New Cold War

There was a lot for me to discover about Japan—especially with regard to the educational system. Uncomfortable with my observations at Hakodate University, some of my acquaintances hastily cautioned me that these experiences did not typify universities at the very top. That may be true, and there are always exceptions even at the lower eschelons.

Nevertheless, too much attention has been given in the literature to the elite schools, and too little attention was focused on what may be the norm. In a nation where 30 percent of the youth population goes on to college (compared to more than 50 percent in the United States, according to the National Center for Education Statistics), even these fiesty young people at lower level universities can be considered representative of the upper ranks in Japan.

It seemed that there was a great deal that Americans missed when they read stories about the Japanese classroom. Time and again I had read glorious lectures in American magazines and newspapers about the reasons why America should be ready to learn new tricks from the Japanese if it was to catch up in the race for economic supremacy.

This race, constantly on the lips of political and educational leaders in both countries, was a race of rivalry between the superpowers. Accordingly, the Cold War with the Soviets was giving way to a New Cold War, which was taking shape in the Pacific.

I came to believe that, upon closer examination, the educational system and the youth of Japan were not what the experts thought them to be. My saddest discovery of all was that this New Cold War of the superpowers was, as with every other war, chewing up and wasting or destroying the lives of many young human beings. And the educational system was the machinery for doing it.

But many of the Japanese were not as tolerant of this New Cold War as were many American commentators. The educational system was under attack from all corners of Japanese society. And the youth were still a rebellious, energetic lot not yet fully harnessed for the race. This was to their credit, even though teachers, such as myself, may not have appreciated this and may well have been uncomfortable with the lack of obedience and calm in the classroom.

This book is intended to give voice to those Japanese parents, youths, concerned citizens, and some foreign teachers who have been striving so hard to make the educational system more humane and more respectful of younger generations.

This book is not to be mistaken as a vehicle for "Japan bashing," because nearly every critical observation contained within this book is one that I have heard the Japanese themselves make about their own educational system. And many of the criticisms could just as well be leveled at the American educational system. Indeed, every word of their attack should be heard by Americans who are bent on reforming the American educational system for the better, instead of simply importing and exporting the same old formulas of student manipulation and control.

Chapter 1 is intended to pique the interest of the reader in the same fashion that my interest was piqued. Newspaper accounts of the death of Toshinao Takahashi caused me to start asking a lot of questions of my students, my colleagues, and my friends.

Chapter 2 explores some of the attitudes typical in publications that seem to be fueling a race between the economic superpowers without really understanding that the purpose of education is to serve people in a free society. Chapter 3 introduces the myriad of rules that regulate every aspect of life for children in Japanese schools. I have also attempted to discuss some of the contradictions that face young people who must obey rules and pursue goals that are not of their choosing.

Chapter 4 is a description of some of the changing, relevant characteristics of Japanese society and how these shape the educational system. Therein lies a discussion of the role of young women, the lack of independent thought, and the lock-step progression of students through their schooling. Chapter 5 details the attitudes toward, and practice of, corporal punishment that is commonplace in the schools and how this is reconciled with laws against such punishment.

Chapter 6 elaborates further on punishment in the school, particularly verbal abuse and intimidation, exercised by teachers in the making of life-determining school reports. Chapter 7 reveals the challenge that has come forth against physical punishment, the debate over rights, court battles, and models of leadership.

Chapter 8 tells the story of young Hirofumi Shikagawa, a boy who was bullied so much that he decided to take his own life. The investigations that followed reveal the extent of cooperation between teachers and bullies in tormenting other students. Chapter 9 examines the widespread phenomena of depression, suicide, neuroses, and examination pressure in the schools.

Chapter 10 shows the extent of student violence in the schools, public reaction to this violence, and the reflection of these controversies in contemporary film and literature. Chapter 11 dissects the myth of Japan as a unified, harmonious, homogeneous society and talks about problems faced by those in Japan who are viewed as different in the schools and elsewhere.

Chapter 12 reaches into Japanese history to show the roots of group responsibility and the dramatic impact of the *goningumi* (five-family system), in controlling the populace, making people fear outward signs of difference. Chapter 13 discusses the steps that are being taken by right- and left-wing groups to push their agenda onto the schools. And Chapter 14 explores a relatively new educational phenomenon outside the regular school system—*juku* (cram schools)—which are growing rapidly. The book concludes with a look at a variety of alternatives that are taking hold across the country, partly in response to disenchantment with the traditional schools.

This book is not intended to be a comprehensive examination of all the positive and negative aspects of, nor a review of the literature on, the entire Japanese educational system. Rather, I have chosen to focus on youth discipline and rights, within the context of other contemporary social issues, because I consider these matters to be fundamental to the future of any nation of people.

I wish to express my gratitude to the many fine people at Hakodate University who struggle valiantly as a sturdy vessel on a great, troubled sea. I am especially grateful to the Nomata, Mizota, Takatsuki, Miyazaki, Shinya, Kawamura, Iguchi, Izumi, Kimura, and Nagahama families and to the members of the NHK English Speaking Society for all the kindness and help they provided during my stay. Also, there were many individuals throughout the country, adults and students, who have assisted me greatly and who have expressed a deep and abiding concern for the development of educational potential in Japan. It would be impossible for me to list them all, and, for the sake of confidentiality, I have chosen to change the names of three interviewees in this book.

Finally, I wish to express my gratitude to Shintaro Ishihara, coauthor of the controversial new book, *The Japan That Can Say No*, because of his enthusiasm for raising public policy debate beyond national borders. Says Ishihara, "Japanese society does not operate in a way that permits us to have honest debates. Even when we are in the midst of a crisis, only external pressure can make us take action" (Takahiko Ueda, "Ishihara Favors SII, Criticizes Super 301," *Japan Times*, April 9–15, 1990).

SHOGUN'S GHOST

1

KILLED OVER A HAIR DRYER

My fellow teachers taunted me with being too soft. I had no alternative but to physically punish the student.

— Kazunori Amamori

The death of sixteen-year-old Toshinao Takahashi first attracted my attention to the secret horrors of *taibatsu* (corporal punishment). When Takahashi's name hit the newspapers, I had already been living and teaching in Hakodate for nine months and had several opportunities to visit primary and secondary schools as a guest.

As the sole full-time, *gaijin* (foreign) professor at Hakodate University, I was frequently invited to visit English classes and contests in the local schools. The treatment and attention that I received was such a sensation that I could well imagine how a celebrity like Tom Selleck would be treated if he strolled onto an American campus.

All activity stopped as kids giggled, stared, and pointed. Some called out "hallo" while others whispered excitedly to friends that a *gaijin* was present. From a visitor's standpoint, the education environment seemed ideal. Students appeared happy and polite.

I had heard so much about the academic achievements and fine discipline before I came to Japan that I did not realize how much of it could be a facade for outsiders. It is always so easy for a visitor to marvel at, and approve of, a benign atmosphere of authoritarianism whenever making a brief sojourn.

No Remorse

My suspicions about the treatment of young people were aroused by an inconspicuous press report concerning Toshinao Takahashi. Takahashi was a second-year student at Giyo Senior High School who had accompanied his classmates on a school trip to the Tsukuba Expo near Tokyo.

At the hotel where the group was staying, Takahashi had been caught breaking a school rule that forbade the use of electric hair dryers. Kazunori Amamori, the teacher on duty, summoned Takahashi in order to have him apologize for this infraction.

With a number of students looking on, Amamori scolded Takahashi, but the boy showed no remorse and refused to apologize. This enraged the teacher, and he started beating Takahashi on the head and kicking him in the stomach.

The youngster dropped to the ground and, kneeling in front of his teacher, attempted to apologize. But the kicking and punching continued until the boy fell unconscious. Takahashi was taken to the hospital where officials reported that he died of head and stomach injuries and shock.

This assault might have passed without any further public attention except for the unusual defense that was taken by Amamori's counsel at the trial. The defense planned to get the charges against Amamori dropped by accusing the school and the entire educational system of gross misconduct.

"They Made Him Do It!"

Amamori had been presented as a teacher who was driven to his misdeed by the demands of colleagues and by pressures of the job. Having just been transferred from another school in the prefecture, he was a new teacher who was eager to adopt the methods that were expected of him on this new assignment.

In his previous post at Gifu Commercial Senior High, Amamori, the son of a Buddhist priest, was reported to have been a kind teacher, and a man who had never advocated, nor used, corporal punishment before. Now, in less than a month, he had been transformed into a killer.

The courts were presented with evidence that, because the National Education Law prohibits corporal punishment, teachers were routinely breaking the law in order to enforce the school rules. In addition, teachers used vigorous physical punishment of students to demonstrate to their fellow teachers a kind of fierce enthusiasm.

Many teachers regularly carried whips around the school grounds. Others toted *shinai* (a bamboo sword) used in *kendo* (fencing), one of the oldest of the martial arts.

"My fellow teachers taunted me with being too soft," Amamori told the court. "I had no alternative but to physically punish the student" ("Verdict Spotlights School Corporal Punishment," *Japan Times*, 3-23-86).

The defense counsel contended that school authorities were responsible for Takahashi's death because they tolerated corporal punishment on a broad scale. Therefore, Amamori was only an instrument in the school's system of punishment, and, they charged, he should not be held solely responsible.

This was a very effective argument since a majority of the nation's schools were in violation of the spirit of the law. If this courtroom tactic was successful, there was every reason to expect that the court might be inclined to dispose of the case quickly and let Amamori off with a simple reprimand.

Forgotten Duty

In the mildest language the prosecution could muster, a four-year prison term was requested for the teacher because "it was clear the accused forgot his duty of giving educational guidance and, in a fit of anger, inflicted corporal punishment that resulted in the death of his student" ("4-Year Jail Term Sought for Teacher," *Japan Times*, 2-20-86). Amamori finally received a lesser sentence of three years for involuntary manslaughter.

The judge explained that Amamori's actions were somewhat understandable because he had probably been motivated by a fear of criticism from colleagues who had wanted him to get tough on the students. Therefore, the judge acknowledged the defense argument that the school environment had contributed to the crime. Since others who were in higher positions of responsibility at the school were not punished, the judge simply used this environmental argument to reduce the penalty on Amamori rather than to expand culpability. The defense strategy had succeeded.

This judgment did very little to change the educational environment. In fact, it may have contributed to the problem by encouraging schools to be more secretive than ever.

Furthermore, education officials were reassured by the court that they would not be held accountable for any general violations of the National Education Law nor for any contributory negligence. This combination of secrecy and lack of accountability would probably contribute to such deaths in the future.

Fortunately, the death of Toshinao Takahashi marked the beginning of a change in the attitudes of people in the media, the teachers' union, the legal profession, and, most importantly, many parents. All over the country, groups were starting to press education officials with hard questions about the conditions that face Japanese youth.

An editorial in the *Japan Times* expressed this sentiment when it declared, "The public has probably become aroused, as the issue has come to assume a life-or-death semblance. And the explanations forthcoming more often than not are inadequately convincing. The root of our dissatisfaction over conditions in the schools is the feeling that we don't know them and therefore cannot understand them" ("Life-or-Death Education," *Japan Times*, 3-16-86).

Blame It on the Family

Conservative elements were quietly blaming schoolyard difficulties on a changing home environment. When I asked a colleague of mine what he thought was at the root of violence in the schools, he simply said, "It's not a problem of the schools. It's a problem of the home and of the family."

It is customary in Japan, a family-centered culture, to view the problems of individuals as being inextricably combined with the responsibilities of the family. As a case in point, I was once informed by a professor at my college that if I had a wife or son who caused someone injury in an automobile accident, I might have to resign from my post at the university.

"After all," he said, "if you can't control your own family, then how can you control your students? We can't have that kind of behavior threatening the reputation of the university."

In the tradition of total family involvement, the family of the teacher who killed young Takahashi tried to resolve the case out of court. It is common practice in Japan for relatives of the offending party to offer substantial sums to the victim or the survivors in order to get a case dropped.

Amamori's wife was designated to visit the home of the dead boy's family in order to offer "an expression of deep remorse and apology." On behalf of her husband, she offered ¥10 million, approximately $80,000, as a condolence. If the money had been accepted, then the charges would have been dropped and both families could have avoided any further publicity.

At first, the newspapers reported that Takahashi's mother refused the condolence money. Then the journalists elaborated on a sensitive tidbit of scandalous family gossip. Takahashi's parents, it turns out, had apparently been separated for the previous eight years. Such family troubles, while currently on the rise in Japan, are still considered rare and somewhat shameful.

Appearances Can Tell It All

The common viewpoint of several of my acquaintances in Hakodate was that Takahashi's "bad" home life had probably caused him to rebel against traditional mores. This was reason enough for them to excuse the teacher from any guilt in this matter.

"When the mother appeared on TV," said a fellow professor, "it was obvious that she probably worked at a bar because of her fancy hairstyle and fancy clothes. And the father looked like *yakuza* (Japanese mafia) because of his bright ring, sunglasses, and manner of speech. Whenever you look closely at a problem like this, soon you will come to the family situation. You always have to dig deeply enough until you get to the family."

For some, the lack of respect that young Takahashi showed to his teacher was the greater crime. Of course, it was unfortunate that the boy died, but what else could come from shameless family circumstances that led, inevitably, to rude behavior?

Said one friend of mine, "Is it any surprise that Takahashi's son died in such a manner? If he had been raised in a better family, he would not have gotten into trouble with his teacher in the first place."

Of course, this idea of associating every student problem with the parents of that student is fallacious. Teachers also had parents, and it could be argued just as logically that every problem involving a teacher also has its roots in the child rearing practices of the teacher's parents.

Certainly there is plenty of room to point an accusing finger at the teacher's value environment. What environment could possibly be responsible for shaping a teacher into a person who was so eager to bend to the pressure of peers that he could kill a young student? Would it have altered the judgment if the teacher had dressed or spoken any differently or if he had been separated from his wife for eight years?

Teacher Is Victim Too

An anonymous letter to the *Asahi Evening News* (3-26-86) protested the sentencing of Amamori. "He [Amamori] should at least be acknowledged as a victim as much as the murdered student is. The true criminal is the prefectural education policymakers and the school authorities. . . .

"I wonder how the ex-teacher will live for the rest of his life. He will have to live for tens of years, expiating the crime of depriving a youngster full of promise and prospect of his life and frightened by the shadows of his act. . . .

"Not only his crime. He must live with the potential crimes committed by the 'teachers' who support 'corporal punishment,' or rather, find a positive meaning in it and bulldoze this devilish act as 'a means of student discipline. . . .

"Giyo Senior High School students, you may be killed tomorrow by the people in a 'holy job' who 'have a true love' for you, and upon whom your parents 'place reliance.'"

2

THE RACE

Bullying, suicides among school children, dropping out from school, increasing delinquency, violence both at home and school, heated entrance exam races, overemphasis on scholastic ratings, and torture of children by some teachers are the result of the pathological mechanisms that have become established in Japan's education system. Without drastic reforms, Japan's education system would not be able to recover to normalcy.

—Ad Hoc Education Council

In numerous articles about Japan, one thing stands out: young people are frequently viewed as a national resource. As such, the young are intended to serve some national purpose. This is usually, but not always, a national economic purpose. And young Takahashi's death might as well be viewed as a casualty in a great global contest for national superiority.

"Like Japan's manufacturing system and its industrial policy, her education has also become a 'challenge,' even a 'model,' for America," says Thomas Rohlen, a renowned expert on Japanese education and author of the book, *Japan's High Schools* ("Japan Education System Sets Model for the U.S.," *Daily Yomiuri*, 5-8-86, p. 7). This view of Japanese schools typifies a growing perception in the West that the education model for the twenty-first century lies across the Pacific.

Hard-working and well-disciplined students, who outperform their Western counterparts in math and science examinations, have frequently been associated with the robust growth of the Japanese economy over the past few decades. Thus, many Americans believe that Japanese schools hold a key to the future of competition in industry and technology.

What is the challenge? Some authorities in the field believe that it is for "our" team to beat "their" team on the economic playing field. Should our team behave the same as their team in order to beat them? And do the popular perceptions of both teams' activities square with reality?

The Economic Race

Pundits in the United States assert that the Japanese team has done well because Japan's economy has obviously prospered. And the economy has been prosperous because of the government's superb policy of shaping and directing the nation's industry. This cooperative arrangement between government and industry, nicknamed "Japan, Inc.," has had many eager proponents within political and corporate circles of America.

At the same time, another group of observers contends that the success of "Japan, Inc." is a myth. Accordingly, they assert that the Japanese economy has been performing well in spite of, not because of, the official policies of Japan, Inc.

This group of revisionists contends that the Japanese economy performed its best in the years when government expenditures and the overall tax burden were by far the lowest among industrialized nations. The Japanese were decades behind Western governments in building the welfare/warfare state, and even today Japan spends only 1 percent of its GNP on the military compared with nearly 6.5 percent in the United States. As the size of government began to grow by leaps and bounds in the last two decades, however, growth rates declined to less than 4 percent instead of the 10 percent annual growth rates of the 1960s.

These revisionists assert that politics played a destructive role in shaping industrial policy. Political manipulation of the economy resulted in inefficiencies and corruption, just as in other nations.

The Lockheed and Recruit Cosmos scandals have demonstrated that Japanese politicians and bureaucrats performed like politicians and bureaucrats everywhere. They fed favors to special interest groups, formed cartels, subsidized decrepit money-losers, threw tax money away on lavish government showpieces, and crushed new entrepreneurs whenever they got in the way.

These policies have left the ordinary Japanese citizens to live in homes that are now commonly referred to as "rabbit hutches." At the same time, influence peddling by the farm sector has foisted rice on the consumer at ten times the world market price. Skyrocketing land prices have become even more outlandish.

Simultaneously, industrial manipulations by the Ministry of International Trade and Industry (MITI) have obstructed competition and price reductions at every turn, making Japan the most expensive place in the world to live. If there is any competitive advantage in the Japanese government–business relationships, declare the revisionists, then it is only because Japanese politicians have been less "bad" than politicians in the West.

Thus, opposite interpretations of the usefulness and proper functioning of government would naturally lead to precisely the opposite prescriptions for future policy, either in Japan or in the United States. The very same holds true in the formulation of educational policy.

Opposite interpretations of the usefulness and proper functioning of government in education would naturally result in opposite prescriptions for future policy. And the difference between those prescriptions could mean the difference between day and night for generations of young people in both nations.

This book is revisionist. Rather than echoing the accolades that many American journalists and educators have been heaping on the Japanese educational system in recent years, often with the intention of importing much of that system, this book uses the critique made by the Japanese people of their own system in order to point the way to constructive alternatives for both nations.

The Educational Race

Having mistaken the causes of Japan's economic successes, American groupies will, not surprisingly, do the same regarding education. Education in Japan is also partly mythical. It is thought to be a kind of ideal system because of successes in the economy.

This is an understandable, natural association. No doubt Native Americans marveled at Spanish education when they saw a mighty Spanish armada sail into the West Indies. And the Japanese of 1853 must have been wildly impressed with American schools when Commodore Perry sailed his black ships into the harbor at Yokohama.

Human awe is an interesting phenomenon. Nevertheless, a couple of decades or even a century of economic growth should not lead anyone to hasty conclusions that perfection has been achieved in education.

The American educational system and culture are fundamentally the same as they were twenty-five years ago when American industry and education were the envy of the world. Now, both industry and education are bemoaned as poor competitors, ailing remnants of a bygone era.

In the 1950s and 1960s, Japan was still struggling out of postwar devastation, trying to overcome the ghastly reputation of wartime atrocities and cheap "Made in Japan" labels. Certainly, Japanese education and culture played a role in rebuilding the nation after World War II, but it could just as logically be argued that these twins, education and culture, played a major role in leading the nation into war in the first place.

If that is possible, then the would-be imitators of Japanese education should take a longer view before passing their legislative resolutions. Is the present system of education in either nation ripe for a repeat of previous wars?

Some publishers seem intent on making it so. The promotional flap on the jacket of one popular book about Japanese education sounds a bit like it is setting the stage for the next global confrontation: "*The Japanese Educational Challenge* by Merry White—

Hers is the first full look at the psychological and cultural shaping of the Japanese child by a society that, from top to bottom, regards any small threat to its educational system as a major threat to its economic survival, its social cohesion, and its world power status and respectability."

On impulse, one might react saying, "Them's fightin' words!" But this isn't what the author had in mind at all.

Commenting on this kind of publicity in a conference at the University of Hawaii, Merry White said, "I once wrote a book about Japanese children which really was about the nature of childhood in Japan. But the publisher insisted on calling it '*The Japanese Educational Challenge*.' It was felt that we might attract people who wanted to confirm their stereotypes about Japan, especially those who believe that the Japanese were in a campaign to win in the schools as well as in trade. But the book is not about threats and challenges. The intention is to use Japan as a kind of mirror, not a blueprint for reform here nor a call to arms" (Merry White, "The Roots of Japanese Behavior," East-West Center, University of Hawaii, 10-14-89).

The major challenge, or threat, to the whole system of Japanese education today comes from within Japan itself, from people in nearly every sector of society who are trying desperately to be heard and to make reforms.

The American Battleground

Some Americans are constantly bellowing that the Pacific War was fought to punish the Japanese for Pearl Harbor and to show them that America was number one. Others thought that Americans were fighting for freedom from oppression—the freedom of individuals and families to choose their own goals in life rather than to have goals crammed down their throats by any ruler.

In the latter sense, the purpose of education is not to show young people how to serve the engine of national economic growth through a disciplined and orderly work force. Rather, education is to provide fertile ground for the pursuit of family and individual goals, which is, incidentally, another interpretation of prosperity.

Rockne Johnson, a philosophical sage, professor, scientist, and erstwhile politician in Hawaii, asserts that this matter of choice is the only real measure of a nation's prosperity. Says Johnson, "Wealth is not measured in things that people have, it is measured by the choices that they have. Material prosperity means nothing to those who simultaneously lose the freedom to decide how to use their lives and the things that they have."

Gumption and Willpower

What do American educators think of choice in Japanese schools? Some of them do not think of it at all.

"U.S. Educators Marvel at Japan's Schools," read the headline of an article by Keith Richburg, a correspondent for the *Washington Post*. Richburg's report captures the sense of enthusiasm that was expressed by a team of U.S. education experts who visited Kyoto and Tokyo in 1985 for a week-long international conference on educational reform (Keith Richburg, "U.S. Educators Marvel at Japan's Schools," *Japan Times*, 10-26-85).

"In most schools," reported Richburg, "children wear uniforms: black pants, white shirts and black high-collar military-looking jackets for the boys; blue skirts and sweaters, white socks and blouses for the girls. Cosmetics are usually not allowed, and teachers in many schools keep a bottle of nail polish remover at their desk, in case some girls attempt a brazen show of individuality."

"When the teacher enters," observed Richburg, "the children, all wearing name tags, stand for a formal greeting: a stiff bow. They usually sit attentively as the teacher lectures, and no one interrupts with questions."

Predictably, it is this kind of regimentation that seems to have impressed the delegation of American educators at the conference. In praising the strict discipline, the fine performance of students on standardized tests, and the relatively high compensation for

Japanese teachers, some of the U.S. education experts expressed a desire to adopt much of the Japanese system in American schools.

"There's about six or eight major shifts we'd have to make," said U.S. Assistant Secretary of Education Chester E. Finn. "Whether we have the gumption to make them at all is the question."

Another delegate, Henry J. Walberg, a professor of education at the University of Illinois, chimed in, "I think it's portable. Gumption and willpower, that's the key" (Keith Richburg, "U.S. Educators Marvel at Japan's Schools," *Japan Times*, 10-26-85).

Individualist Ideals

While these Americans have been marveling at the educational practices in Japan, the Japanese have been busy eyeing the West. One newspaper declared, "Premier Praises U.S. System of Education," during one of former Prime Minister Yasuhiro Nakasone's visits to the United States.

Nakasone was intrigued with the American educational system, and he established a special Ad Hoc Education Council to consider overhauling the system in Japan. In its early reports, this Education Council was utterly brutal in its criticisms of Japanese schools, and it battled for reforms that are drawn from an appreciation of the Western sense of individuality.

In April 1986 the Education Council summarized the crisis in Japanese schools saying: "Bullying, suicides among school children, dropping out from school, increasing delinquency, violence both at home and school, heated entrance exam races, overemphasis on scholastic ratings, and torture of children by some teachers are the result of the pathological mechanisms that have become established in Japan's education system. Without drastic reforms, Japan's education system would not be able to recover to normalcy" ("Gist of Education Council's Proposals," *Japan Times*, 4-24-86, p. 2).

The Education Council said that the most important reform is to do away with the "uniformity, inflexibility, closedness, and lack of internationality," which are thought to be at the root of education ills in Japan. The council members hope to accomplish this by "respecting the dignity of individuals, individuality, freedom, self-discipline, and individual responsibility" ("Panel Urges Educational Reforms," *Japan Times*, 6-29-85).

Curiosity of Zombies

Says one council member, researcher Shigeru Kawabata, "I see very little to recommend the Japanese education system, other than high SAT (Scholastic Aptitude Test) scores in mathematics and science. Japanese children are beaten into molds by a system that crushes individual expression and creativity."

James J. Kilpatrick came back from a visit to Japan thoroughly impressed with the long hours of instruction: 8:30 A.M. to 5:00 P.M. on weekdays and half a day of classes on Saturday, for a total of 243 days of school a year compared with 180 in the United States. Kilpatrick was convinced that this would surely give the Japanese superiority in the business world fifteen years hence. So why not lengthen the school year in the United States? (James Kilpatrick, "Japan Shapes Tough Future Leaders," Universal Press syndicated story, *Boulder Daily Camera*, 1985.)

This additional quantity of schooling does not necessarily mean that the result was any better for the individuals involved. According to educator Masako Sugiyama, "When Japanese children are going to school the equivalent of two months longer each year than American children, it is little wonder they are scoring higher on SAT's."

Intense pressure to perform in lower grades leaves young people burned out by the time they reach college level. Says Kawabata, "Our universities are academic wastelands, and the students attending them have the intellectual curiosity of zombies" ("Japanese Education Overrated," *Arizona Republic*, 4-13-87, p. 12).

Even the corporate leadership in Japan, which is supposedly served most by the Japanese model, is highly critical of the nation's educational system. Konosuke Matsushita, elderly founder of the mammoth Matsushita Electric Industrial Company, has long advocated the elimination of half the university system.

Believing that much of the education was not worthwhile and better served by other institutions Matsushita proposed the selling of Tokyo University assets, which he said would save the nation a half billion dollars per year. On his own initiative Matsushita even started his own institute, the Matsushita Seikeijuku.

Norikazu Kabayama, former vice president of Marubeni (Canada), Ltd. and head of his own marketing consulting firm today, admires the private prep schools in America—to which many American families have tried to escape. "I believe that Japan can learn a lot from the way the American schools are managed and conducted," says Kabayama. "Prep schools contain practically no *koonai booryoku* [interschool violence], *ijimekko* [bullying] or bribing of teachers. There may be isolated instances here and there, but certainly not to the extent that it exists in Japan.

"There is also no cheating in exams in the prep school and," states Kabayama, "students do not face the cut-throat competition to succeed in order to be admitted to a particular college" (Norikazu Kabayama, "There's More to Learn from U.S.," *Japan Times*, 11-10-85).

The Grass Is Always Greener

What do the Japanese think of their own education system? Well, just as in the United States, that depends on who you talk to, what they are focusing on, what their motives are, and whether or not they are dependent on the status quo.

One might generalize by saying that people within the educational establishment are less critical of their own system than those on the outside. And, in the midst of an "education crisis" nearly everywhere, people tend to believe that the grass must be greener in other countries.

Of course, borrowing from abroad has always been easier than instituting new ideas that upset the fundamental nature of an established educational structure. But there are a few who try the latter.

Says Kawabata, "I don't think anybody has found the perfect system yet. But if we don't keep trying, then I am afraid Japan will be left in the dust by the time the twenty-first century gets here."

Voicing firm agreement, an editorial in the *Asahi Shimbun* (4-6-86) declared, "The real problem confronting us now is that the present school system has reached a dead end. The reason is simple: schools are still trying to follow outdated practices despite the different circumstances that surround today's youngsters. And to make matters worse, schools are being forced to fulfill roles they could never have handled in the first place.

"A radical overhaul," continued the editorial, "is a must if the education system is to be freed of the present excessive reliance on schools. There is no reason why education, in the broad sense of the word, should not take place more in the home, local community, and society at large."

This gloomy, pessimistic view of education in Japan contrasts sharply with many American journalists, officials, and scholars who have been preaching the virtues of the Japanese educational system.

3

RULES, RULES, RULES

Forty years ago, it was "war" that murdered all those young lives. Today, it's the rein of "control" that's murdering us. We've been turned into sheep, with no spirit of resistance, by society, adults, and schools.
—Jin Ogasawara

Schooling is much more of an all-consuming way of life for students in Japan than it is for students in the West. Not only do they spend the equivalent of two months more per year in class than do Western students, but nearly every minute of their lives, even outside of school, is ruled by school officials. There is intense pressure to perform well on high school and college entrance examinations so that students can qualify for the best of careers in the corporate or bureaucratic worlds.

When young Toshio came home from junior high school one day, he immediately went up to his room to study. His mother explained to me that it was always like that for him and for his buddies who were equally serious about passing the exams.

At first it sounded to me like Toshio was a well-disciplined kid and that he could surely get his homework out of the way early in the evening. Then he could enjoy dinner with his family and maybe a few hours of television or recreation with his friends. Not so.

Toshio's mother explained that her son went directly back into his room after dinner, and he studied until 1:00 or 2:00 A.M., with a one-hour TV break permitted. School rules did not allow him to

get together with his friends in the evenings, and he avoided the
family, especially his father, like the plague. It seems that he and
his father never spoke without getting into a fight.

Cramming

Still, there was not much time for Toshio between school and
home. Attendance at *juku*, (cram schools) every week absorbed
five to ten additional hours from his evenings and weekends. For
some, this obsession with scoring well on the national entrance
examinations could demand many more hours of study, especially
in the years just prior to the examinations.

The average Hakodate University student went to *juku* about
three hours per week per subject. But students from very good high
schools typically attended up to fifteen hours per week. Natsuo
Oshima, my brightest student, told me that he usually studied six
hours a night, six times a week, and twelve hours on Sunday, for
a total of nearly sixty hours each week. This included ten hours at
the *juku*. Said Oshima, "Of course it was a lot, but those at the
highly competitive Tokyo high schools do even more."

"Pass with four, fail with five," was a common phrase among
the students, referring to the number of hours of sleep that one must
be limited to in order to pass the examinations.

The pressure to do well on the examinations seems to be at an
all-time high. The enrollment of junior high pupils in the *juku*, has
risen threefold in the past ten years despite rapidly rising tuition
fees.

Ken Kageyama, a professor of physical education studies at the
Aichi University of Education, asserted, "Children are being
forced to cram knowledge into their brains while they do not know
why they have to study. Schools have become something like
prisons."

Befitting this description, students are often scheduled to do the
cleanup of school grounds and classrooms—and they are frequently punished for "escaping" these chores. It may seem virtuous
to have the students doing chores around campus instead of

custodians, but virtue is only derived from the existence of choice, and these students are offered little or no choice.

As youngsters jumped to bells and commands, 80 percent of the youths at municipally run schools in Okazaki city found that virtually all remaining free time was taken up with sports organized and sponsored by the school. These teams had practices in the mornings, after school, Saturday afternoon, Sundays, and even during summer and winter holidays. Those not enrolled on sport teams were expected to be in other clubs.

Said Kageyama, "Children do not have time to play. It is as if club activities and homework assignments were used to restrict children's freedom." Continued Kageyama, "I believe that *kanri kyoiku* [rigid school regimentation] has come into existence because parents and citizens have completely left education to the schools" ("When 'Controlled' Education at Schools in Aichi Goes Awry," *Japan Times*, 4-23-86).

Absentee Fathers

Kageyama certainly is correct in his assertion that the father plays a very small role in educating his own children. In a nation where real fathers are working ten to twelve or more hours a day, six to seven days a week, coaches become a kind of surrogate father for the students. This is especially true in Hokkaido, for instance, where the basketball season runs all year. It isn't unusual for fathers to regularly work late into the evenings and more on Sundays.

One friend of mine in Hakodate, Okada, provided a good example of the salaryman who has an intense work schedule and little time to play. As manager of an employees' cafeteria at the Boni Department Store, he bought fresh vegetables and fish in the morning market every day, seven days a week, starting at 6:00 A.M.

Okada said that since his job did not require him to entertain business clients in the evening, he left work after a twelve-hour day at 6:00 P.M. With little time remaining for the family, he still took two hours, twice a week, to practice English at meetings of the English Speaking Society.

When asked how much time he got off from work, he said one day per month, except in December when the store was too busy. And how did he spend that day? "I usually play golf," said Okada.

My student, Oshima, once recalled a time in his youth when he saw a stranger coming into the house. He asked his mother who that man was, and she replied that it was his father. He responded, "What's a father?"

Upon hearing this, Oshima's father felt embarrassed. The man was determined to become closer with his son by taking the boy along with him on his business errands the very next day.

So, Oshima was packed into the car and, at the first stop, his father told him to wait in the car a few minutes while he checked on a couple of clients at a used car dealership. When the man returned, ten hours later, young Oshima had already cried himself to sleep in the back seat of the car. They did not spend many of their days together after that.

Mama as Agent of the State

Stories about fathers are endless, and all seem to reinforce what students tell me are the "Four Hatreds" in historic Japan: Fire, Thunder, Earthquake, and Father. While this alienation is understandable between father and son, could Kageyama also have been referring to mothers when he said that "parents and citizens have completely left education to the schools"?

This seems to be at odds with current Western interpretations of the role of the educationally minded mother, the "*kyoiku mama.*" She is often described as a woman who has little else to do except to dote over the child in every conceivable way, prodding the youth toward educational excellence.

The only way to reconcile these views is to understand that *kyoiku mama* is an educational extension of, or agent of, the school and the state. After all, the *kyoiku mama* is most renowned for her efforts at encouraging her child to fit into the mold, the established pattern of education, rather than to venture into educational frontiers on his or her own, defiant of the educational establishment.

The best evidence of this "mother-as-agent-of-the-state" syndrome, hardly unique to Japan, is the way that enthusiastic mothers panic when they believe that their children might be violating some *kosoku* (school rules). It is then most apparent that the mothers are the frontline enforcers of the school rules.

When a student is found to be in violation of the rules, the teacher first calls the mother to scold her for any infractions. Hiroko Sato explained that when her son was caught without a plastic lining for the collar of his uniform or when his pant legs were one centimeter too long, she was the first to receive a reprimand. The only way to appease the school was for her to traipse down to the school, make the repairs, and offer a string of apologies.

In another case, during a school trip to Nara and Kyoto, a teacher discovered that one student was wearing trousers that were a few centimeters narrower than allowed by the *kosoku*. The teacher immediately telephoned the boy's mother long distance to scold her for allowing this breach of the rules.

Deeply ashamed, the mother grabbed a new pair of trousers and hopped on a bullet train for the 370-mile trip to Nara. Both mother and son are reported to have concluded the event with repeated, tearful apologies for their misconduct.

This event inspired one youth, Takeshi Hayashi, to write a book entitled, *Fuzakeru na, Kosoku!* or (*Give Me a Break, School Rules!*). The book is based on his own experiences and research, from the perspective of those forced to go through the system. More than 10,000 copies have been sold ("Young Author Jabs Rigid School Rules," *Japan Times Weekly*, 7-11-87 p. 4; "He Who Fights the School Code Loses," *Asahi Evening News*, 6-15-88, p. 6).

The book inspired a flood of correspondence from some 4,000 readers who sent in reports of their own experiences. These were published in *Fuzakeru na, Kosoku!, Part 2* and *Fuzakeru na, Kosoku!, Part 3* has already gone to press.

Trivial Conformity

In the book, Hayashi describes many cases of onerous regimentation that are designed to ensure rigid conformity in virtually every aspect of life. Much of this regimentation is focused on the most trivial details of dress and behavior.

One girls' high school in Tokyo checked on students to see if they were wearing the regulation underwear. Those with polka-dot or colored panties, instead of standard white, were forced to stand at the front of the class while the teacher denounced them as having the "mentality of bar hostesses."

In other cases, girls were punished for using the wrong color rubber bands on their projects. Others were prohibited from entering a classroom in groups; instead they were forced to line up neatly before entering.

Recalling his own junior high school experiences, Hayashi told of one teacher who forced a girl to sit strait-backed for seven hours because she came a few minutes late to class. Another teacher used to strip boys to the waist and beat them with a steel-pipe chair.

One day at a junior high school in Tokyo, about twenty students were told, on the morning of their departure for a school trip, that they would not be allowed to go on the trip because there had been some violation of the rules. The teachers amused themselves by refusing to tell the students what rule had been broken. Finally, after repeated requests for an explanation, one boy was told that his shoes had only five pairs of eyelets instead of the requisite six pairs ("The Peculiar Dress Codes of Japanese Schools," *The East*, November–December 1988).

The Japan Bar Association (JBA), after a survey in 1985 of rules and regulations in 535 junior and 293 senior high schools, reported that most public high schools and junior high schools across Japan impose exacting and complicated rules and regulations on virtually every aspect of a student's personal, social, and academic life, both on and off the school grounds.

The report cited a middle school in Aomori Prefecture that "orders its students to march to music in neat lines, eyes turned toward the teacher on a platform at the morning roll call. In standing at attention, toes should be angled at 45 to 60 degrees and fingers should be extended straight with the palms touching the body. In saluting, the upper body should be inclined forward at 30 degrees and held rigid before resuming an upright posture in a smooth manner."

The JBA was critical of schools that molded students' uniform behavior and deprived them of their right to make even the smallest personal decisions. A high school in Shizuoka-Prefecture was cited as ordering its students to "obtain permission from your parents and then from homeroom and counseling teachers before you attend a primary or middle school alumni meeting."

This kind of rigid performance may be all right for a centuries-old tradition of tea ceremony, but the JBA did not believe that it was appropriate to the more than 17,000 hours of compulsory education for the young. Particularly sensitive to issues of due process and the guarantee of rights, the JBA noted that none of the schools surveyed gave students a chance to offer an excuse or to have a hearing when accused of breaking the rules.

This was hardly the preparation that was essential to the development of a democratic society. After all, democracy is best served when individuals have at least a fundamental appreciation for rights in general ("Schools 'Too Strict' on Students: Report," *Daily Yomiuri*, 9-2-85).

Surprise Inspections

Schools may have 200 or 300 meticulous rules, written and unwritten, which govern student behavior twenty-four hours a day. Some schools require young people to carry a little book with them at all times that lists the formal rules of the school and provides space to record each student's compliance with those rules. Any teacher may stop a student at any time and ask to see his or her record of behavior from the first day of entry into classes.

Frequently one can see signs prominently displayed at the entrance to school buildings that resemble "wanted posters." These posters show two pictures, profile and back view, of a male or female student wearing the permissible hairstyle.

These and other rules governing appearance are strictly enforced at the school gates or by surprise inspections at school assemblies in the gymnasium. When going through the door, students must be in line with their hands clasped behind them while teachers, sticks in hand, commence inspection.

One teacher at a private girls' school in Hakodate explained "the wet down" inspection this way: "Without warning, all the girls are told to line up in the gym. Then a teacher goes down the rows with a bucket of water and a comb.

"When a wet comb is run through a student's hair, you can tell if she has had a permanent. You can't tell by looking whether or not the students have a perm because some of them have naturally wavy hair. So the teachers devised this way of uncovering violators. Those that violate the rules are pulled aside and have their hair cut on the spot."

At another high school, the principal refused to allow pictures of several girls to appear in the school album because of their nonconforming hairstyles. Instead, pictures of flowers were prominently featured where the girls' photos should have been, thus highlighting the voice of disapproval. And in Kanagawa Prefecture a junior high girl was forbidden entrance to the school for nine months prior to graduation because she had worn a skirt that was longer than permitted.

At one junior high school, I asked the girls why they were not allowed to have their hair permed. They explained that school officials told them it would distract them from their work if they were busy attending to their hairstyles.

I reminded them that the chairman of their school system had his hair permed, along with several of the school administrators and teachers. Did this "attention to hairstyles" prevent these administrators and teachers from doing their work? The girls giggled. They seemed to recognize the hypocrisy, but, unlike Hayashi, these girls somehow felt that it was not their right to be upset about it. What harm is there in a little hypocrisy?

Contradictions

In most countries, people recognize that there are problems in the educational system, but there is little agreement over what to do about it. Some people would like moral education and more respect for the individual. Others would like less competition and more personalized attention from the teachers. And there are many who say that the parents must become more involved in school affairs.

They may all have valid points, but what usually escapes attention are the contradictions that students are compelled to cope with through most of their early school life. This can lead to serious difficulties in the development of values and ethical behavior.

The kind of life that young people see exhibited by adults often stands in sharp contrast to ideals in life that youth are encouraged to pursue. Consider, for example, something as simple as the rule against smoking and drinking. Almost every school in Japan threatens to expel young people for doing what half of their teachers and parents do every day.

When one walks around the faculty offices one can find an ashtray on nearly every desk. (While it is relatively rare for women to smoke in Japan, a very high percentage of men smoke, and an overwhelming majority of the teachers are men.) In a teacher's home, one can almost always expect to be served sake, beer, and whiskey in succession throughout the meal.

In asking my students at the Kyoiku Daigaku (teachers' college) whether or not it was all right for students to smoke cigarettes, they responded unanimously "No!"

Why?

It is harmful to one's health. (The most common response.)

Because I can't smoke, I don't want anyone to smoke.

It is bad for one's intelligence.

Smoking bothers me. It is troublesome to nonsmokers.

Young bodies are not grown up enough to smoke.

It is a nuisance.

We can live without cigarettes.

It stunts growth.

An adult can take responsibility for his actions but a child can't.

Students are weak.

We can't live long if we smoke.

It's against the law.

I then asked the same classes, filled with teachers-to-be, if it is all right for teachers to smoke cigarettes. Seventy-six percent replied "Yes!"
Why?

The teacher's body is already grown up. (The most common response.)

Teachers are adults.

Teachers are mature.

It's legal.

Since it is his responsibility, he can do as he likes.

Teachers' smoking has nothing to do with students.

If teachers can't smoke, no one will want to become teachers.

It is a matter of personal freedom.

It's bad for teachers, but they love it.

Smoking calms frustrations. Teaching is nervous work.

A teacher should hide his smoking.

The teacher has a right to smoke, but he should not in front of his students because it leads students to smoke.

The Power of Seniority

The young are told that the rule against smoking was made for the protection of their health. Why, then, do the rules change after a certain age? Is it because health is of less concern to older people? On the contrary, it is the elderly, not the young, who are obsessed with staying healthy. Surely the elderly are even more vulnerable to habits of poor personal hygiene.

However, the rules against smoking and drinking really have little to do with health. Rather, the rules have everything to do with power. The rules change for older people because they have the power, and young people do not. Adults have had more practice at rationalizing their own behavior, and they have the power to present a hypocritical set of guidelines for the young.

Because young people learn more through imitation than by lectures on virtue, they learn much that was unintended by their teachers. Many students become cynical about the logic and motives of rules, and they discover that ethical principles can be twisted to suit one's power and status.

What kind of behavior might a teacher be eager to write down in the student's record book if a student is lucky enough not to be outright expelled? This is what a few hundred students told me they should be guarding against in junior and senior high schools:

No dancing, except folk dancing

No part-time job

No jewelry, usually with the exception of watches

No car or motorcycle driver's license

No smoking, anywhere

No hair dye, perm, or unusual hairstyle

No rock 'n' roll music

No alcohol

No hair below the eyebrows

No staying out after 6 P.M., or 5 P.M. in winter (junior high), 10 P.M. (high school)

No staying overnight at a friend's house

No changing the color, shape, or design of one's uniform

No taking magazines to school

No black leather jackets

No more than 5,000 yen ($38) on one's person

No stopping on the way to or from school

No going to coffee shops or tea rooms

No sunglasses

No beard or mustache

No leaving books at school

No chewing gum or candy

No standing on the threshold of a teacher's office

No makeup

No kissing, sex, or marriage

No riding a car to school and, for some, no bicycles

No wearing of special buttons

No color ribbons, socks, or other private clothes

No stepping on the back of one's shoes

No squeezing or coloring the school bag

No tattoo or losing a finger (manifestations of gang membership)

No "escaping" from, or running away from, school

No going to discos, bars, or cabarets

No hitting

No grease in the hair

No manicure

No knife

No massage parlors

No running in the school hall

No gambling, visiting pinball (pachinko) parlors or, for some, bowling

No carrying of cigarette lighters

No entering pornographic movie theaters

No outdoor shoes in the school (Hokkaido)

No wearing a sweater or jacket in class without permission

No tardiness

No lending money or textbooks

No participating in a studio band

No talking or noise

No eating snacks at school

No tearing one's diploma

No traveling without school permission

It was an interesting coincidence that these rules prohibited behavior by young people that would have been acceptable if practiced by the teachers themselves. Consequently, it was no surprise to me that 95 percent of the junior high school girls that I surveyed said they did not like the rules that were imposed on them. In fact, the only teacher that they were enthusiastic about was one who was the least conformist and who did the least to enforce rules.

Social Repression

Mrs. Sato described for me the public junior high school regulations that governed her son. Students were not allowed to enter the front entrance of the school, that was reserved for the teachers. Student toilets were specially designated for use, north or south, depending on the grade level of the student. This is a form of early training in seniority privilege that is not unlike the practice of segregation elsewhere in the world.

Sato recalled how a teacher once scolded her for allowing her son to go to school with pants that had belt loops in the back that were crossed instead of parallel. She apologized profusely.

Boy/girl friendships were carefully monitored as well. Sato told me that one time she was pleased to see her son become interested in a girl at school. The girl even began wearing a ribbon in her hair to be more attractive.

But the teacher warned them both against paying too much attention to each other and to their personal appearance. The girl was told to get rid of the ribbon, and Mrs. Sato's son felt compelled to ignore the girl. This monastic-like scrutiny of social behavior has left the young people of Japan repressed and extremely immature in their relations with other youths of the opposite sex.

One time I brought a couple of classes of men and women from different colleges together in order to plan some social activities. Beforehand, both groups had expressed excitement over the idea. But when they met, I was stunned by the inability of either group to carry on any conversation in the presence of the other. Week after week they sat in muted silence until we just abandoned the whole idea.

Indicative of the problem awaiting these youngsters in later years was The Marriage Man Academy. This academy in Osaka was recently established as a kind of finishing school for men who do not know what to do around women—an increasing problem as women are more frequently taking on jobs, waiting longer to marry, and becoming more independent from their parents in choosing their husbands.

Said Satoshi Noguchi, manager of the academy, "up to about ten years ago, if a woman wasn't married, she literally couldn't afford to eat." But now that women are more economically independent, according to Noguchi, they can be more picky, and men have to learn some manners and "special tricks."

Junya Hori, a thirty-four-year-old student at the academy, commented, "When I talk to girls, conversations always end after 'hello'." What is one of Noguchi's special tricks?

"Always sit to the right of a woman. When she sits to the left, she hears everything you say through her right ear. Any words that are heard through the right ear go to the left side of the brain—the emotional side" ("School Offers Shy Guy New Lease on Love," *Japan Times*, 4-18-89). Supposedly, a woman using her intelligence rather than her emotions would not give this turkey a second thought.

Like the Air

Common literary fare are the comic books. Widely read by men and women of all ages in Japan, comics are piled by the dozens in coffee shops and sold by the millions at rail station kiosks. These are rife with surreal, sadistic, and extremely brutal caricatures of sexuality. The same college men who devour comics by the dozen, are frequently unable to make even the most rudimentary social contact with women.

The development of such social skills is still relatively new, and perhaps unnecessary, to many Japanese. Fifty percent of the marriages are still by *omiai* (arranged through introductions) and recent trends show that this percentage is increasing.

One young professional, a graduate of one of the top universities, confided to me, "I was forced to marry my wife. She was introduced to me by my senior in the company. To refuse marriage would be very disrespectful to my senior.

"We have one child now and," he added with a touch of sadness, "my wife always goes to bed with the child at 8 o'clock. She said that it helps my son to sleep better. I can't say that it helps my sleep much. I rarely get home until 10:00."

Those who are discouraged from social contact in their youth seem unable to fully develop an emotional rapport with spouses in later years. The woman leads a life at home with the children, which is almost completely isolated from the life of her husband.

I once invited the college faculty, all of whom were men, to my house for dinner, insisting that they bring their wives. One woman told me later that it was the first time that the wives of the faculty had met each other. Although I tried to explain that it was to be a buffet style American dinner, the men remained seated, waiting to be served by their wives.

Said one middle-aged, fairly progressive professor, "I usually do my research at home until 1:00 A.M. and I might sleep with my wife once a month. My wife is like the air: you notice its absence, but you don't think about it much when it's there."

Still, these are more tolerant times than in the old days. Before World War II, boys and girls could be punished simply for extending a greeting to any person of the opposite sex, even while walking downtown. Said one elderly woman, "We always had to keep our heads bowed and pretended not to notice when passing boys whom we knew on the street." While noticing the opposite sex is not explicitly against the rules today, much is done to prevent the opposite sex from being very noticeable.

Closely Monitored Living

Typically, hairstyles and uniforms at many schools were expected to meet exacting standards, without deviation or adornment. To prevent "misunderstandings," boys had to submit an "application for different attire" when the uniform was being sent out for cleaning. And those with naturally wavy or curly hair were advised on the day of registration to notify the school officials so that they would not later be accused of getting a perm (George Fields, "Cultural Insularity—Unofficial Part of Japanese School Curriculum?" *Japan Times*, 7-2-87).

A private girls' high school in Okayama holds a haircolor check every month to make sure that every girl's hair is properly black. Of the 1,500 enrollees in the school, 131 were judged to have 'red' hair upon first inspection and were ordered to undergo compulsory dyeing at a cost of ¥4,000 ($29).

Hiroki Takaki, the hairdresser appointed to dye the girls' hair, said, "I have taken care of fifteen girls sent to me in March and April and two of them had naturally brownish hair. I felt a bit sorry for them but had to dye their hair anyway, since 'a bad law is still a law' " ("School Goes Way Beyond Splitting Hairs," *Japan Times*, 5-28-89).

The costs of school regulations could mount in other ways as well. In 1986, the requisite book bags, clothing, notebooks, and pencils, which along with the typical home desk averaged $1,162, were considered to be essential for the first-year student in primary school, according to a survey by the Tokyo Metropolitan Government Citizen and Cultural Affairs Bureau ("Cost Per Pupil Set at 151,108 Yen," *Daily Yomiuri*, 2-6-86).

Students generally do not have lockers at school for their textbooks and personal belongings, so everything must be carried to and from school every day in expensive black leather backpacks (elementary school) or briefcases (junior high). If a teacher finds books lying around school, the books might be confiscated and the student hit the next day while being scolded in front of the whole class.

The untrained eye of the foreigner might not be able to tell the difference between one school's $150 briefcase and another school's $400 briefcase. But there is usually some slight, mandatory distinction in the cut, stitching, buttons, buckles, or snaps.

Defying the Rules

In a show of defiance, some rebellious youths conform to the letter of the law by carrying the mandatory bags, but only after soaking them in water and ironing them flat to make it crystal clear that there could not be any books inside. In response, the schools made rules outlawing the "squeezing" of school bags.

After World War II, there were similarly defiant gestures by students who flattened the backs of their shoes so they could be slipped on more easily without the extra effort of tying and untying them every time. Teachers recoiled at this, saying that shoes were too valuable to be broken down in the back; the practice was outlawed.

Students told me of six classmates they had known over the years who joined the *yakuza* because of a sense of alienation from the rest of society. These students would sometimes show up at school wearing black leather jackets, dark sunglasses, and a shortened finger. A well-known practice of the *yakuza*, and something of an amusement to outsiders, is the requirement of rookie criminal gang members to cut a finger off at the joint as a sign of loyalty or as punishment for some significant blunder.

Frightened by the presence of *yakuza* members at school, school officials "cleverly" attacked this trend by outlawing black leather jackets, sunglasses, and even the losing of fingers. The list of rules grew, and student alienation became greater.

With increasing affluence, the tide of defiant behavior has been impossible to stem, and the schools have tried to enforce rules on a greater range of items, that is, jewelry, cars, briefcases, even money. Some authorities have forbidden students ever to have more than ¥5,000 yen ($36) with them at school, threatening confiscation against offenders.

Of course, the teachers missed the point of the rebellion altogether. The students were rebelling against the schools, not their shoes, briefcases, and fingers.

4

CHANGED YOUTH, UNCHANGED INSTITUTIONS

One of the reasons, and probably the greatest reason, for the pathological phenomena occurring in the schools today, including violence and "bullying," is the gap between the changed values and attitudes of young people and the unchanged orientation of the older generation.

—Ikuo Amano

Ikuo Amano, a specialist in educational sociology at Tokyo University, claims that today's prosperity has left young people less hungry for economic success than their parents. And he contends that Japan's century-old "credentialism," the reliance on academic ranking to determine wages, prestige, and power, is winding down.

"Already there is a growing number of very well-educated college graduates who will not receive promotion to managerial positions, or cannot even find white collar jobs," said Amano.

"Of course, there are still many children who will study very hard to pass the entrance exam of a prestigious school in hopes of gaining a high position in society. And school education takes it for granted that children are strongly oriented to upward mobility. As a whole, however, such children are becoming a minority."

Concluded Amano, "One of the reasons, and probably the greatest reason, for the pathological phenomena occurring in the schools today, including violence and 'bullying,' is the gap between the changed values and attitudes of young people and the unchanged orientation of the older generation. The educational system and institutions, which are maintained and run by the latter, have changed little" (Ikuo Amano, "The Dilemma of Japanese Education Today," *The East*, January–February 1989).

Indeed, conservative institutions attempt to tighten their grip the more their purpose disappears. According to a 1987 national survey of 2,698 junior high school teachers, the rigidly enforced rules in Japanese schools are supported by 86 percent of teachers. Ninety-five percent of these teachers believed that disorderly attire was akin to mental disorder, and the same number concluded that "non-allowed hairstyles and delinquency are interrelated."

Another 68 percent thought that the school should control the kind of socks that students wore, and 38 percent felt that the gloves allowed should also be controlled. Two-thirds of the teachers believed that going to "amusement centers" should be prohibited and that schools should still enforce bans on students going to coffee shops (Peter McGill, "He Who Fights the School Code Loses," *Asahi Evening News*, 6-15-88).

A somewhat conflicting view of teacher support for the rules was uncovered by a more recent survey in Gifu Prefecture. A group of local school teachers' unions, the Conference of the People for Better Education conducted a survey to find out how widespread the *kanri kyoiku* (rigid school regimentation) rules were. Eighty percent of the teachers in this survey said that their schools had strict regimentation as described in the previous chapter.

Interestingly, more than 70 percent of these teachers said that such controls were unnecessary, but they were reluctant to openly challenge the system. Instead, they joined the few teachers who believed in *kanri kyoiku* and helped to promote it.

Many of the teachers in the survey believed that both parents and students had adapted themselves to the regulations. This was not, however, confirmed by a poll of the parents and students. The survey found that both parents and students were opposed to the strict rules, especially those rules that prohibited students from such things as talking while eating lunch ("Teachers, Parents Express Doubts About School Rules," *Japan Times*, 4-16-89).

One might conclude that there is either a considerable lack of communication between these groups or that there is a small, but highly intimidating, group of teachers that persists in the enforcement of unpopular rules.

Spy Duty

Students are required to be in school at a specific time, they cannot leave before, or stay later than, closing without permission. They must carry their ID cards with them at all times, even outside of school. This tracking system is necessary for the routine inspection role of teachers who are detailed to roam various hot spots in the community, looking for insolent youths.

A friend of mine, a foreign teacher at a girls' high school, recounted that the farewell address to the student body one summer consisted of a reading of an endless list of rules. Once the girls were gone, the teachers, who were expected to be on duty all summer long, drew up a schedule of assignments for spy duty.

Every teacher was expected to do undercover patrol in front of Boni department store, pretending to be shopping for two hours, on four occasions during the summer. The faculty practiced, and taught this deceit by example from 4:00 to 8:00 P.M. daily.

The more enthusiastic teachers would patrol the campsites while taking their own holidays. The male teachers could be expected to interrupt their own bar-hopping to peek into the discos and cabarets, forever on the prowl.

All the teachers were encouraged to ride the buses every now and then in order to keep alert for any noisy misbehavior of students that might reflect badly on the school. "Because the kids were wearing badges and uniforms, the school believed that its reputation rested with every kid's actions," declared my friend.

According to Christian Huggett, regional correspondent for the *Japan Times*, teachers in Okazaki city drop by students' homes at 10 P.M. to investigate whether or not a student is still studying. If the student's room light is off the teachers "will enter the house, take the student to his room and force him to study. They may also search the student's desk for prohibited items and take down any posters of youth idols in the room."

"Teachers inspect students' luggage before school excursions," says Huggett, "to see if their underwear is the regulation white. Students are also inspected at their destinations, as they disrobe for bathing." Parents rarely object, and those who do face stiff opposition from the whole community (Christian Huggett, "Okazaki Boy Struggles for Independence from School's Close-Cropped Conformity," *Japan Times*, 2-27-90).

Looking over One's Shoulder

Thus, the students spent the whole of their waking lives looking over their shoulders. But it did not prevent many of the girls from being quite blatant about their liaisons with boys. "Students are often not even discreet," commented one teacher. "Sometimes they walk hand-in-hand down the busiest street in town, not even worried about getting caught."

On the average, two or three students were caught every day on some violation at this one school. If a girl was seen with a boy, walking together or sitting in a car or cafe, she would be suspended for four days and required to come before all the teachers with the routine, formal, tear-filled apology.

"The school held two 'ice cream meetings' to discuss the crimes of two students who were seen buying ice cream on the way home from school. Well, that's against the rules," commented the teacher sarcastically. "The faculty never held such a serious meeting when a student attempted suicide. When a girl jumped from one of the school buildings it was all hush, hush!

"In the more serious cases, such as a girl having sex with a boy, all fifty-two teachers at the school were called into a room where the offender faced them and recounted the full details of her 'crime'," said the woman. "The teachers know everything that happened because the kids tell them everything. Wouldn't you tell if you were in the kid's shoes and being yelled at so long by so many?

"As long as I can remember," she continued, "I'm the only one who ever voted against the recommended punishment. Even then the school president gave me a scowl that made me shudder. For Japanese teachers, the president has enormous power and control over their whole future."

"But I'm a *gaijin* and out of here if I don't like it. I think the kids know about my position, too. Many times they've been overcome with guilt and tell me in confidence of every cigarette they ever smoked. They don't dare say that to one of the regular teachers."

She explained that a girl could get a month suspension if she went to a *rabu hoteru* (love hotel or "no-tell motel" for trysts) and stopped just short of intercourse . . . otherwise it would have been immediate expulsion. "This isn't much of a deterrent to the girls. A lot of them go to love hotels and could care less about getting kicked out."

"School Is Stupid for Girls"

"One of my students put it bluntly," recounted the teacher. "'School is stupid for girls. It doesn't matter if I study or not since I can't do any better than become a clerk anyway.' Love or romance seems to be the only excitement for so many of them.

"I'm getting tired of hearing them say that their life is practically meaningless. When I ask them to tell me what their hobby is, they say, 'to listen to records' or 'to sleep'."

Throughout the world, women have been particularly damaged by educational systems that have contributed to the suffocation of individual aspirations and the romance of meaningful, chosen values and ideals. Life styles are changing, more as a result of outside influences than from any substantial change in the educational system. This has not been without some foreboding among men, who can be heard to say, "Women and stockings have both become stronger since the war."

The opportunities for women are growing slowly, but generally speaking girls from mid-level high schools have little or no chance for a career in the corporate world in Japan. As a consequence, some have found lucrative alternatives, notably the age-old alternative for women who desire independence but have respectable doors slammed in their faces. This side door is seldom discussed, either inside or outside of Japan.

The World's Oldest Profession

One graduating student went to her teacher's house and lingered around the whole afternoon. "It was obvious that this girl had something serious to tell me," said the teacher. "So many girls come to me because I'm probably the only adult friend they have who won't be visibly shocked by anything they tell me.

"I noticed that she had a really nice bracelet on and, just trying to get the conversation going, I asked her how she got it since she's not allowed to have a part-time job. After a great deal of nervous hesitation the girl explained that she hires out for sex whenever she needs money.

"She goes over to the old fort district and calls a number that's posted in a phone booth. She waits about half an hour and then a man drives up and takes her to a love hotel. She gets about ¥20,000 ($143)."

"How common is this?" I asked.

"The girl told me the names of sixteen other graduating seniors who regularly did the same," said the teacher. "She refused to tell me about the girls in the lower grades. They were even more involved, but she didn't want to say anything while they were still at the school."

The incidence of youth prostitution is surely much greater in metropolitan areas like Tokyo. Along the major thoroughfares or train stations like Shinagawa or Shinjunku, one can find nude photos and telephone numbers of dozens of girls pasted on poles or listed in little booklets that are stacked in telephone booths.

The antiprostitution laws are not strictly enforced, except as they sometimes apply to minors or illegal immigrants. The hypocrisy of enforcement became most apparent in the summer of 1989 when it was publicly acknowledged that many prominent politicians, including Prime Minister Uno, kept paid mistresses for years at a time.

Young women can be arrested and taken into protective custody simply because of official suspicion that these girls exhibit "a tendency to commit a crime in the future" ("Number of Minors Taken into Custody for Prostitution Increases Dramatically," *Japan Times*, 1-30-86). In 1985 the Tokyo Metropolitan Police Department (MPD) announced a dramatic increase (up 262 percent) in the number of these young wards who acknowledged having sex with men for purposes of entertainment or curiosity, or to meet living expenses.

This trend was viewed with growing alarm by Shigeru Nozawa, director of the Juvenile Division of the MPD. Nozawa was convinced that the number of girls mentioned in official reports was only the tip of the iceberg.

Previously, said Nozawa, girls had been taken into custody following raids of *yakuza* brothels. But recently they were finding more and more girls who were hanging around game centers and discos waiting to be picked up. Half of them had initiated the sexual contact with men.

Little Room for Mistakes

Young people can see through the hypocrisies of contemporary society. They know that adults are also complicated human beings when it comes to attitudes toward sex, manners, appearance, and values. Unfortunately, the urge to keep these issues hidden makes it all the more difficult for people to learn from the actions of others.

"Why don't the teachers try to talk with the students to understand the reason they behave badly? Controlling the students by strict rules is no education," said author Takeshi Hayashi (*Japan Times Weekly*, 7-11-87, p. 4).

According to Hayashi, "It's crazy. In or outside school, teachers are pressuring children, not treating them as human beings. Children have to be allowed to make mistakes and learn from them" (*Honolulu Star-Bulletin*, 7- 27-87).

To some of the *gaijin* (foreigners) living in Japan, this insulation from mistakes and from real learning is an ever-apparent phenomenon that leaves the Japanese unable to assert control over their own lives. Education in Japan has left the Japanese dependent on schools and on officials, says Alexander Kent in a letter to *Japan Times*, 6-20-87.

Kent observed that "while the Japanese are ferociously schooled, they are woefully uneducated." By way of explanation, he noted that the Japanese study English for six years or more, yet they are unable to speak more than a few words of the language after all that time.

Kent was particularly disturbed by the apparent inability of many Japanese to learn anything on their own initiative without a school. He commented that the Japanese compulsively sought schooling in every realm of human activity: swimming schools, tennis schools, brides' schools, office workers' schools, picture takers' schools, and even test takers' schools.

Kent's letter was inspired by news reports of "yet another murder suicide involving a Japanese woman and her children." The woman killed her children and then took her own life rather than follow her husband to his job in Tennessee where it appeared that there would be no Japanese school. Her tragedy could have been averted, declared Kent, if she understood that "all life is not school and that there are ways to learn that are clearly superior to any taught in Japanese classrooms."

Lockstep Progression

This observation concerning the association of schools to the necessity of learning seems as appropriate to Americans as to the Japanese. For few schools anywhere seem to be designed to foster genuine independence of thought and action; if they really did, youths would then have independence whenever they were ready to choose it instead of being compelled to sit through the same droll routine until the requisite number of years has passed.

"Before the war," explained Kazu Tomisawa, a woman who grew up in Hakodate, "smart students could leap up grades if they performed well. But now, even at the university, all students progress strictly at the same pace."

"How did this change come about?" I asked.

"General Headquarters [GHQ of the American occupation forces] imposed the present system of education on Japan after World War II. It was fairly easily accepted because people assumed that American victory proved that it was the best education system in the world.

"The new democracy said that everyone was equal. So the Japanese interpreted that in the traditional manner that 'different people' is wrong. Everyone was to get exactly the same schooling. Prior to that, education was accessible to a student who tried hard and had ability. Even a peasant's son could go up to the highest levels. Teachers and rich merchants would sponsor them and take care of them. But a dull student, even if his father was rich, did not go up to the top.

"After the war," Tomisawa continued, "all were equal, so all want children to go up to the top even if they were dull students. So the pressure was great at all levels to succeed.

"Before, the purpose of education was knowledge and real power. Now the purpose is just a diploma and passing the university examination. The students are exhausted when they graduate and forget what they are studying for.

"Now the teachers themselves are the first products of the new system. They are only idealistic, not proven by practice and time in the culture. It's really an unknown path," concluded Tomisawa.

All this was confirmed by Toshio Murata, a professor at the Yokohama College of Commerce, "Not only could students skip a grade up, but prewar education emphasized ethics. In fact, a great portion of the teacher's education was spent in teaching teachers how to behave. Now, through the powerful Nikkyoso [shortened form of Nihon kyoshi sokai—teachers' union], they have become more interested in raising salaries than in teaching students.

"Prewar examinations were all essay, looking for depth in student responses. Now, half the exam is multiple choice and the examiners only look for a regurgitation of facts. The students cannot establish their own framework of choices beyond standard questions," declared Murata.

Exploding in frustration one day, one foreign teacher from a girls' junior high said, "If I tell my students to write about anything, they sit there motionless. They can't write. But if I give them a topic, then they can start. It's the same with drawing."

Individualism: A Strain on the System

Explaining the rationale for the uniform pace of student promotion, Masatsugu Kimura, a professor at the Kyoiku Daigaku (national teachers' college), replied, "Students don't move at separate paces, it's true. But this is for a good reason. The law decides how many students there will be in each class. It is presently set at forty-five for all levels. All lessons are the same for all students, and it is very difficult to change the class or homeroom teacher. Of course, it is also very difficult to change from a bad teacher.

"However, this is well-suited to the situation in Japan while the American system is not appropriate in Japan," commented Kimura. "The same lessons are given to all students in the same class. Because of racial homogeneity and groupism there is a tendency to give the same education to everyone, with the optimistic belief that every student can get a certain level of education knowledge. Fundamentally, we don't believe the individualistic view that some are genius and some are slow. The majority of students are standardized at mid-level, generally.

"If the American system was adopted, where students were free to choose classes and level of ability, this would create a great strain on our capacity . . . buildings, teachers, everything. The Japanese system operates very effectively at a very low cost, whereas the American system is very high cost."

"Thus," said Kimura, "by moving everyone along at the same rate, they can all choose their direction in life at the same time. They only have one chance."

It would appear that Douglas MacArthur's vision for Japanese education was quite different from the result.

5

PUNISHMENT

In training dogs and horses, they receive a treat whenever they behave, and they are whipped when they don't. The same stance should be taken with children. Children are animals being taught to be human.
—Kinji Kato

"At Ueno Station, I saw a familiar scene," wrote Jin Ogasawara, a nineteen-year-old student from Tokyo. "That of junior high students with their identical clothes, hair, and shoes on a school trip. They somehow struck me as lacking in vigor and spirit and gave the impression of having just come out of a concentration camp. They were an absolutely and totally controlled group.

"I, too, during my junior high days experienced having my personal rights and individuality suppressed and eradicated," declared Ogasawara. "Teachers pound into the student's heads that 'one acting on his own will be a great nuisance to everyone else,' and in the end no one can do anything by himself. Also they lecture students to 'always govern your actions with common sense,' thus leaving students incapable of thinking and acting differently from other people. Everything is done in groups. Like in the military there is no self, and no individuality to be recognized.

"And after having had such an education ruthlessly enforced on us, our generation is now being criticized and condemned. We're labeled the new breed, characterless, listless, unfathomable, etc. But those of us being criticized now were, in reality, 'murdered' beforehand. Forty years ago, it was 'war' that murdered all those young lives. Today, it's the rein of 'control' that's murdering us. We've been turned into sheep with no spirit of resistance by society, adults, and schools" (Letters to the Editor, *Asahi Shimbun*, 6-22-88).

Japan Bashing Japan

How is this control imposed? How are the rules of uniformity enforced? If the "crime" is as severe as being late to class, not doing one's homework, talking in class, or even associating with a student who has a bad reputation, then it is possible that the student will receive a hard blow across the head or face.

In 1986 Professor Morikatsu Imabashi, of Ibaraki University, reported the results a survey of 272 students in the education department, in which he asked them about the incidence of corporal punishment in the lower grades. The students reported that they had all been physically punished and that the average had been 23.5 times throughout their education.

Imabashi made his report in Tokyo at the "Study Meeting on Children's Human Rights and Corporal Punishment," which was attended by fifty scholars and lawyers. Punishments that resulted in pain were such things as being forced to sit or stand upright for long periods of time, being hit with the open hand, a fist, objects, or feet.

The students witnessed twenty-seven cases where victims were so severely beaten that they had to be treated at the school clinic or nearby hospitals. This appeared to reveal a sharp rise in the severity of the cases reported compared with three years earlier ("Poll: Kids Get Punished 23 Times as Students," *Daily Yomiuri*, 1-20-86).

When asked why the punishments had been given out, one student claimed that a friend of his in the first grade of primary school was slapped twice for not returning the cleaning equipment to its proper place. Sixty-four percent of the students in the survey said that they thought the punishments were "terrible," and 40 percent said they "hated" those teachers or "would like to kill" them.

This seems to confirm the findings of my own surveys among students at Hakodate University, Kyoiku Daigaku (a teachers' college), a junior college, and a junior high school and of former students still living in the community. Of 227 pollees, 89 percent reported having been hit by teachers over the years, with some being battered hundreds of times. The response to "How many times were you hit by a teacher?" was as follows:

None	12 percent
1–5	19 percent
6–10	16 percent
11–20	20 percent
21–30	9 percent
31–50	8 percent
51–75	5 percent
76–100	4 percent
100–150	4 percent
151–300	3 percent
301–500	1 percent

One student, who told me that he had been hit as many as 500 times, said that he had come into the school on one of those rare occasions when students were allowed to transfer. Thus, he was considered an "outsider" and bore the constant brunt of attacks by teachers and students alike. He assured me that the 500 hits only counted those delivered by teachers.

"They Were Hurtin' "

Students were apparently hit with whatever was handy. A foreign student who was playing a scrimmage basketball game between Hakodate University and Yuto High School came up to me shaking his head in bewilderment. I asked him what was wrong.

"Since I'm so tall, the high school coach assigned two of his best players to cover me really tight. At one point, I feinted right and dodged around them on the left. The coach was furious.

"He called the two players over to the sidelines where he grabbed each of them by the ears and smashed their heads together with all his might. I could hear the crack all the way across the court. Those two guys bravely fought back the tears, but they were hurtin'!"

In questioning students about the punishments they received, I asked if they had been hit (a) very hard, (b) hard, (c) easy, or (d) with a soft tap? At the same time I demonstrated the degree of force in each with a slap of my hand on the blackboard or desk . . . using all my might for "very hard." Forty percent said that the hardest they had been hit was "very hard," but on average the hits were:

Very hard	10 percent
Hard	51 percent
Easy	28 percent
Soft tap	9 percent

The frequency and severity of the hitting varied according to several factors. Female students were just as likely to be hit as male students, but it appeared that female teachers were far less likely to hit students than were male teachers. And students from more competitive schools seemed to be hit less than students from schools that were on the lower rungs of the academic ladder.

Even Baseball Bats

I was quite surprised to hear a man at the NHK English Speaking Society (ESS) tell me that in his school years he had even been hit with a baseball bat. To his surprise, his fourteen-year-old daughter sitting next to him at the meeting piped up saying that she had been hit with a bat, too.

So I asked my students what did their teachers use for hitting. It was almost anything.

Open hand	38 percent
Fist	21 percent
Kendo bamboo sword	11 percent
Foot	8 percent
Book	7 percent
Eraser	4 percent
Chair	3 percent
Baseball bat	3 percent
Other	12 percent

The "other" category included anything that was handy: compass, weighing scale, tennis racket, baseball glove, bucket, slipper, bottle, elbow, and chalk. One student reported being on the receiving end of a high kick with a spiked shoe.

"Where were you hit?" I asked the students. Usually the hits landed on the head or face.

Head	34 percent
Face	33 percent
Hip	6 percent
Shoulder	6 percent
Leg	6 percent
Back	4 percent
Stomach	4 percent
Buttocks	3 percent
Other or everywhere	7 percent

When asked to explain why they had been hit, these were some of the responses:

I brought a comic book to school.

I couldn't answer a math problem.

I spoke ill of my teacher.

I told my teacher, "I hate you!"

I drank on a school excursion.

I couldn't do division.

I was chattering with others.

I injured my friend.

I was late for a meeting.

I talked about the teacher's teaching.

I talked in a meeting.

I didn't straighten up the room.

I stayed awake after lights out on a school trip.

I didn't bring a dictionary to English class.

I obstructed the lesson.

I talked back to the teacher.

I wore the wrong clothes.

I made a baseball error.

I missed a test.

I was cheating.

I escaped from class.

I slept in class.

I broke a tool.

I was eating and drinking in class.

I was playing cards in class.

I drew a picture of the teacher's face.

I escaped from swim club.

I forgot homework.

I couldn't answer a question.

I peeked into the girls' changing room.

I ate lunch early.

I ran in the hall.

I played hooky.

I forgot my textbook.

I was smoking.

I had my hair permed.

I read a magazine.

The teacher thought I broke a rule.

No reason.

The teacher was in a bad temper.

The whole group was hit.

I made a hole in the desk and drank juice through a straw in the hole.

I stole something.

I was fighting.

I injured someone.

I hit a teacher.

None of the incidents listed above are examples of behavior for which an adult would expect to be hit. If someone tried to hit an adult under those circumstances, extremely unlikely in Japan or elsewhere, then the one doing the hitting would be considered childish and he or she could be taken to court for assault.

Adults who were guilty of the above-mentioned offenses might expect some form of nonviolent disciplinary action, but surely there would be some procedures for a hearing. Youths, on the other hand, cannot expect any sort of hearing before they are punished. Guilt is established solely by the teacher's judgment or whim.

Breaking the Law to Enforce the Rules

Young people are ruled by an entirely different and much harsher set of standards than are adults. The irony of all this is that the teachers themselves are breaking the law when they mete out these kinds of punishment.

Article 11 of the School Education Law specifically bans *taibatsu* (corporal punishment). This punishment is defined as violent assault, such as hitting or kicking, and nonviolent punishment, such as forcing children to sit or stand in one position for long periods of time.

Despite the law, there appears to be broad public support for various forms of physical discipline. A poll by the Japan Youth Research Institute shows that 55.7 percent of Japanese parents approves of corporal punishment, versus 29.9 percent in the United States. ("Junior High Class Sizes Here Are Double Those in the U.S.," *Asahi Evening News*, 2-15-86). And a survey by the *Asahi Shimbun* concluded that 81 percent of the populace believe that such punishment may be inevitable ("Fifty Percent Blame School Bullying on Problems with Families," *Asahi Evening News*, 3-24-86).

To illustrate a point, I first asked my class of teachers-to-be at Kyoiku daigaku what they thought of warfare. They all agreed that war was terrible and had to be avoided at all costs. Why? Because violence is wrong, and it destroys people's lives.

Then I asked them what they thought about the idea of teachers hitting students. The overwhelming majority said that it was all right. Why? This was a sampling of the responses by those who thought it was all right:

It should happen because education needs something to fear.

It should be through love.

If the student was bad, it was good to hit, depends on the case.

If the teacher hit, then of course it was for good.

Bad behavior deserves bad treatment.

It will make people try to have a good personality.

Because students get angry.

The teacher gave a warm mind to the hitting.

It was educational.

It is none of my business.

And those who did not like the hitting gave these responses:

If the student was good, then the hitting was bad.

Hitting is not needed, it's very bad.

I never like the hitting of students.

Teachers shouldn't hit.

It seems like the way of the old Japanese army.

I think it's a bad teacher who hits.

The teacher is weak.

I dislike violence.

I think it is only done by hysterical teachers.

Then I asked them if it would be all right for the principal of the school to beat a teacher who had violated the School Education Law by practicing corporal punishment. Of course none of these future teachers agreed with that. But at least there was a long pause as a few of them began to realize the contradiction they had been expressing. It was probably the first time that many of them had been called upon to apply the same rules of behavior to both the powerful and the powerless.

Practicing What Is Preached?

In general, students are continually reminded that bullying is wrong. Teachers tell them this in assemblies. Even floats at parades preach the terrible inhumanity of bullying others.

"Intimidation and violence are serious violations of the basic tenets of human behavior," say the school officials over and over again. "Men and women have brains which must be used to set humans above the brutish behavior of animals."

But students frequently experience a lesson from the observation of teachers that is diametrically opposed to the rules against bullying. Some teachers browbeat and humiliate students in front of their peers. If that is not enough to induce submission, a teacher might give the slow learner a rap across the head.

The astute pupil comes to the conclusion that the lesson on decent, reasoning human behavior does not apply to people with great power. Even the rules that exist to restrain teachers from hitting students are of no consequence if there are no other adults around who object.

In following the pattern of a few belligerent teachers, a clever student bully might learn to avoid recriminations by giving excuses. And the best excuse for any bully is to explain that his or her actions were really motivated by "concern" for the victim. It is an excuse that could be readily adaptable to many walks of life as the student grows up.

One concern of the schools is to prepare young people for life in the world of work. Here, again, contradictions abound because there is almost no resemblance between the classroom and the workplace.

In fact, the authorities seem intent on keeping young people from going near a place of business so long as they are enrolled in school. Employment laws and school rules leave the impression that real, paid work could be as harmful as cigarettes or drugs.

Students are admonished to study hard for letter grades, paper stars, and a pat on the back. After a dozen years of grueling competition, they may expect to be rewarded with a post in some prestigious company or government agency. Perhaps they might rise to the most esteemed of professions, that of public school teacher, where competition ceases altogether.

In the United States teachers may be given three years' probation before their job becomes permanent. In Japan, teachers receive tenure in the first year, and there is no parallel to the security that follows. Only what are considered extreme situations could force a teacher to resign in Japan: stealing, murder, trouble with women, homosexuality, polygamy, fighting, mental disease, embezzlement or, I was told, even pregnancy.

Preparing for Democracy

What is the example that stands before the students eight hours a day, 240 days out of the year? Would teachers be motivated to work diligently for nothing more substantial than pencil marks in a gradebook? Do teachers provide students with a model of competitive enthusiasm while pursuing vaguely defined goals that are not even of their own choosing?

Students are told that school prepares the young for a role of self-determination in a democratic society. Yet the pattern of governance they have to follow in the classroom is strictly autocratic.

The young do not get practice in questioning authority, which is the very essence of democracy. Instead, they are expected to practice taking orders from an indisputable master.

And that is exactly the way it should be in such a training ground, according to a company executive in Yokosuka City in Kanagawa prefecture. Said Kinji Kato, "The mass media is embarking on a full-scale campaign against corporal punishment. One television program even had children criticize such punishment by their own standards. But teachers are human. I feel they are unable to maintain professional standards under these conditions.

"When I raised my children," continued Kato, "I asked their teachers to use corporal punishment if necessary. In training dogs and horses, they receive a treat whenever they behave and are whipped when they don't. The same stance should be taken with children. Children are animals being taught to be human.

"The American families in my neighborhood are very strict with their children, sometimes to the point of corporal punishment. We shouldn't criticize corporal punishment and degrade the whole education system if we want our children to support democracy and follow society's rules.

"Although brutality should be eliminated, we must trust the teachers and let our children receive the professional, loving whip of their instructors. It is about time," concluded Kato, "that amateurs stop depriving the teaching profession of its pride" ("Tolerate the Loving Whip," *Asahi Evening News*, 12-3-85).

Democratic Training?

Kato's comparisons of the treatment of children with that of animals inspired a terse response from an American educator and former probation officer who was living in Tokyo. Says Andrew Hughes, "Kinji Kato's support for corporal punishment in the schools could come only from one who knows nothing of educational psychology and who was probably raised under the old militaristic regime of brutal discipline; it is the way of the fascists, not of adult-minded democrats who place the stress on human values and reason. And to say that training dogs and horses requires the whip and the same stance should be taken with children puts human intelligence and will at the level of animals.

" . . . Mr. Kato's whole idea of corporal punishment is a betrayal of the teaching profession and violation of the rights of children.

"What right have we because we are physically stronger to violate the rights of the child, with what he calls a 'loving whip'? There is no such thing.

"I hope that this old brutal militaristic mind," declared Hughes, "can be eradicated from the educational life of Japan's children. This in itself would be a step in the right direction, helping to end bullying and violence in schools."

It is interesting that Kato would draw a reference to American practices in order to justify those in Japan. And if Hughes rankled at Kato's suggestion that Americans were supportive of corporal punishment practices, he would be surprised by surveys of American public opinion. Corporal punishment is broadly permitted in America, although it is more restrained by the likelihood of a parental and legal battle.

Corporal punishment is banned in only eight states and some-what regulated in fourteen more (David Ramirez, "Spare the Rod . . . ," *The Arizona Republic*, 3-23-86). And a Houston poll indicates that the support for corporal punishment in America runs deep. Seventy-seven percent of the teachers, 60 percent of parents, and 49 percent of students favor corporal punishment ("Paddling: Still a Sore Point," *Newsweek*, 6-22-87).

Disappointing as this may be to Hughes, democracy among adults has little to do with a respect for children's rights. Democ-racy, of course, means many things to many people. Most often it is simply a counting of hands, not an assurance of rights. And in the process of counting hands, the hands of young people do not count.

6

LESSONS IN VIOLENCE

I was appalled by the deliberate cruelty with which some teachers rubbed salt into children's wounds.

—Michiko Nagahata

In 1987, fifteen-year-old Mikinori Tsuchida was sent to a private boarding school in Chichibu District where he tried to escape the day of his arrival. Tsuchida's mother notified the principal, Rinzo Kagawa, who then organized a party of five other students to forcibly return the boy to the school. When they found Tsuchida, they forced him into a car and brought him back that night.

The next morning the gang, which had grown to thirteen students, acting under Kagawa's orders, punished Tsuchida so that he would not try to escape again. They pushed socks into his mouth, bound his hands and legs with vinyl tape and beat him on the buttocks with a metal baseball bat for the next nine hours. Kagawa then confined Tsuchida to a room on the second floor of the institute where he went into shock and died. The prosecutors demanded a five-year prison sentence for Kagawa, but this was reduced because, according to the presiding judge, it had not been proven that the beatings had caused the boy's death ("Ex-reformatory Chief Receives 3 1/2-Year Term in Fatal Beating," *Japan Times*, 2-15-89).

School of Terror

In another case, the *Daily Yomiuri*, with headlines similar to what would have been given to an international incident of terrorism, declared "3 Yokohama Teachers Led 'School of Terror' " (1-19-86). Said the paper, "Three teachers of a Yokohama middle school are accused of at least 20 cases of violence against students over the past three years. . . ."

The *Yomiuri* story focused on the new, city-operated Shimoseya Middle School that was the subject of a lawsuit by irate parents who accused the teachers of brutalizing their children. The bold headlines for this event were well justified.

The suit claimed that one third-year student was kicked and beaten by three teachers for cheating, despite persistent pleas for forgiveness. During the next two weeks, the boy required medical treatment for a cut tongue and bruises to his face that prevented him from eating.

In another case, four third-year students were beaten and kicked by the same three teachers while other teachers stood around watching. One boy, who was knocked down and had his neck and face trampled on by a teacher, later became mute and autistic. The youths were being punished for staying home and boycotting the schoolwide sporting events. It seems that they had long suffered abuses during these contests and did not wish to put up with it any longer.

Two years earlier at the school, a student had his skull bashed in with a baseball bat by an advisor to the sports club. And other belligerent teachers helped to intimidate everyone into silence by regularly warning students that they had better keep their mouths shut if they wanted a good report for their advancement to a good high school.

These three teachers were largely successful at keeping an array of sordid practices hidden from the outside. But one youth finally could not take the pressure any more and tried to kill himself. Only by failing at his suicide attempt was his father finally able to learn what was going on at the school.

It was in this same manner, through botched suicides and severe injuries, that the case at Hanno Nishi Middle School in Saitama prefecture became known. There a social studies teacher beat two second-year students on the back of their heads with a two-foot long, vinyl chloride pipe.

It was reported that the teacher, Yukio Aoki, frequently used this pipe to punish students. In this particular case the boys were being punished for forgetting to bring their textbooks to class. Presumably a beating across the head with a pipe would jog their memory.

One of the two boys resumed his activities after the beating, but when he returned home he began to suffer from severe headaches and was taken to the hospital where he was diagnosed with a brain hemorrhage. Less sensational, but more ominous, a case like this raises questions about the kind of "social studies" training that the students were getting year in and year out under the tutelage of this kind of teacher ("Teacher Beats Boy with Pipe," *Daily Yomiuri*, 4-24-86).

The Silence Unravels

As violence in the schools was being reported more regularly in the media, a growing number of parents seemed to become encouraged to ask questions and to talk more about what was going on. Soon stories were filtering out about schools all across the country.

At one Tokyo symposium on corporal punishment and youth rights, nearly one hundred parents, teachers, doctors, and students came to hear the horror stories of student victims. As with a ball of yarn, once a strand comes loose, the whole begins to unravel.

One Japanese mother at the symposium recounted how her son had been subjected to three years of abuse by a teacher. The youth had been kicked, beaten, and dragged around the school yard. His head was hammered against a goalpost, and he was thrown onto a garbage dump and jumped on.

"It all started when my son skipped soccer practice one Sunday to go fishing with a friend," said the woman. "Ever since then the teacher continued to pick on him for no explicable reason.

"Early in 1983, the boy was beaten so badly that he had to receive extensive medical treatment," she explained. "There were alarming symptoms of anxiety and depression. I went to the school and demanded a meeting with the teacher. He refused to see me. Instead, I was told by the principal to take my son out of the school if I had any complaints" (Masaru Nishigato, "Violence at the Teachers' Hands," *Asahi Evening News*, 11-27-85).

The woman finally decided to go to court, a very unusual course of action in Japan where few people will use the law to challenge the authorities. Her reluctance is understandable considering the potential financial cost, public embarrassment, lack of sympathetic treatment, and years of delay that she could expect in the court-room.

The teacher in this case was eventually fined ¥30,000, then equivalent to $146, for assault and battery, but never offered a word of apology.

A few bold parents do register complaints, and a few school officials have given out various forms of administrative punishment to the offending teachers. As a result of media attention in recent years, the number of teachers across the country who are disciplined for inflicting corporal punishment has been on the rise. According to an official of the Tokyo education board, the reports of corporal punishment have increased because parents have been trying harder to bring teacher violence out into the open.

Sadistic Practices

It seems that students are also becoming more aware of their right to a more peaceful education. Sixteen former students of a high school in Mie Prefecture filed a suit for a quarter of a million dollars in damages resulting from violence by teachers and other senior students at the school.

All of these students finally left the school and went to other prefectures to finish their education, but they felt that the school had to bear some responsibility for the suffering that they had undergone. Responding to the pressure of continual beatings and harassment, one of their classmates committed suicide by jumping from one of the school buildings and others set fire to a building with the hope of being allowed to go home.

"There was no true education at the school," declared the plaintiffs. "The students were in danger of being hurt in school. We were forced to quit school." Ironically, the school had been formed in 1985 under the guiding principle that teachers and students should walk hand in hand ("16 Former Students File Damage Suit Against School for Alleged Violence," *Japan Times*, 3-1-86).

Sadistic practices of teachers took on more imaginative forms in Hyogo Prefecture where a home economics teacher used pins to prick the abdomens of thirty boys and girls over a two-day period. This thirty-eight year veteran of the school system had been teaching sewing to fifth graders.

When the students failed to use their marking pens correctly, the teacher pricked them until they bled. Parents finally protested and questioned the teacher about the practice. The woman explained that she wanted to teach the children "that wrong use of marking pens would hurt" ("Teacher Allegedly Pricked 30 Pupils as Punishment," *Japan Times*, 11-21-85).

An elementary school teacher discovered that eight boys and five girls had forgotten to bring their books and calligraphy materials to class. As punishment for forgetfulness, all these children were forced to remove their skirts and pants in class. After an hour in the cold November weather, they were finally allowed to put their clothes back on ("Extreme Lesson in Forgetfulness," *Mainichi Daily News*, 12-5-88).

And there was the Nishinomiya Kita teacher who is said to have forcibly placed a connected propane hose into the mouth of a student when he refused to reveal the names of other members in a "delinquent" student's group. Justice Minister Hitoshi Shimazaki told the members of the Diet, Japan's parliament, that this kind of punishment is an everyday affair at many schools in Mie Prefecture ("School Punishment to be Checked," *Japan Times*, 10-24-85).

The Revered Sensei

Unlike the situation in western nations, the status of the *sensei*, (teacher) in Japan is highly revered. And when a teacher is brutal to a student, this reverence translates into a tremendous fear and timidity among both students and parents. Who would dare to challenge the authority of one who has such prestige in the community and who wields such power over a youth's future?

Parents in these circumstances can seldom get help from the school principals because the officials are frequently more concerned about shielding the reputation of their schools. Reputation is vital to the successful recruitment of students, to the strength of community support, and to the prestige of the faculty and administration within that community.

In Japan, community status is much more important than salary or bonus. After all, the status of one's employer plays such an important role in determining what social clubs one might be invited to join, what families would be considered marriageable prospects, and many other forms of influence upon the near and distant future.

Parents sometimes become immobilized when it comes to confrontations with the authorities or with other people's children. Parents who side with their own children in these battles are in a distinct minority.

An educational specialist from the Hakodate Board of Education, Shooji Teraoka, reported to a Parent-Teachers' Association meeting one year that parents usually believe that any trouble at school, whether from bullying or corporal punishment, is usually the fault of their own child. Parents responded that the causes of trouble suffered by their children were as follows:

	Sons	Daughters
Can't help, fashion, fact of life	18 percent	7 percent
Other child's fault	29 percent	50 percent
Teacher's fault (meaning the teacher lacked power or control)	12 percent	14 percent

	Sons	Daughters
Can't help, fashion, fact of life	18 percent	7 percent
Can't do anything because children are like that	6 percent	2 percent

The result, said Teraoka, is that as young people get older they are less and less likely to tell their parents anything about the trouble they are having.

When a crisis at school is unavoidably revealed, that is, because of injury, there are some parents who would like to do something about it but feel that they cannot. The parents who oppose corporal punishment in general, or a specific application of the punishment, rarely criticize the school openly because the school plays such a powerful role in the determination of a student's, and family's, future.

Said one student victim's mother, "If you want your child to get good reports so they can attend a good senior high school or college, you don't go make enemies with the faculty."

Michio Nakamura, president of the Okayama Bar Association complained recently that a girls' high school was violating students' human rights with strict regulations mandating that all students had to have black hair. But the parents were afraid to express any criticism.

One student at the school was born blond and had to dye her hair six times at the school. Her father pleaded with a news reporter, "Please don't make a fuss since she has to go to college next year." Thus, continued the reporter, "implying that any criticism of the school might have an adverse effect on her academic record and harm her prospects for admission to college" ("School Goes Way Beyond Splitting Hairs," *Japan Times*, 5-28-89).

Student Reports

Naishinsho (student conduct reports) were originally intended to relax the obsession with test scores by allowing teachers to keep records of a student's all-around performance, socially as well as academically. Unfortunately, vindictive teachers have twisted these reports into a weapon for the enforcement of obedience to orders (Peter McGill, "He Who Fights the School Code Loses," *Asahi Evening News*, 6-15-88).

These secret student reports are sent to high school and university admission committees, which increasingly rely on them to screen out students who might cause problems. Masatsugu Kimura, a professor at the teachers' college in Hakodate, commented in an interview, "A teacher's confidential report about a student's attitude plays a very important function when many high schools and colleges are selecting students. So, students must be very subservient and obedient to their teachers.

"Grading is done on a scale from A to I," said Kimura. "If a student gets an E or F, it means that it will be very difficult for him to succeed to good schools. If he has a low report, then he is destined to go to a low level high school. It is separate from the examination and based on the teacher's opinion and school grades. The teacher can write anything and it is not seen by the students or their parents.

"The recommendation letter in U.S. schools is given much less emphasis. In Japan, the report has great influence on the student's course."

The fear that parents and youth have of these reports and the teachers that compile them is usually difficult for Americans to fathom because of the multitude of routes to success in the United States. In Japan, however, there are fewer routes to success, and the teacher holds the key.

A law professor from Doshisha University in Kyoto, Yoshinobu Tai, commented, "The schools are very competitive and the parents tell their children that doing bad things will mean that they cannot enter a good company and they cannot get a good woman. It puts a particularly heavy pressure on boys. In Japanese society there can only be one failure and then one can never come back to the same status. One failure and he must spend the whole of life at a lower status."

Professor Tai continued, "Now so many young people are so calm. Children just stay home, studying or watching television, and won't go out. People don't know why they are so passive."

Transferring from school to school is very difficult because it puts the student at a severe disadvantage in his educational career. He is treated as an outsider when going to a new school, and there are considerable obstacles to gaining acceptance by teachers and other students.

This is a wrenching problem for many fathers in Japan, fathers who are expected to move frequently with job promotions but who do not wish to have their children suffer the handicap of transferring schools. The term that is used to describe this phenomenon is *tanshinfunin*, meaning an unaccompanied transfer apart from one's family.

"It sounds like cruel punishment, but almost always the transfer amounts to a career boost," commented the editors of the *Japan Times* (6-28-87). "But does the family togetherness have to be sacrificed? The distressing reply most often given is yes, for the children's smooth schooling must come first.

"It has already grown to the status of a recognized major social problem. One of the latest polls, all dire in their findings, discovers that two years is the maximum separation from his family the typical male worker can stand." The editors warned, "Now, women workers are becoming more subject to transfer away from their families, too."

An executive of the Boni department store in Hakodate described to me the hardship that he had been going through over the previous decade. He had taken various posts all over the globe and was never able to take his family out of Tokyo because he felt it would jeopardize his son's chances at a top-level college and job.

For his son to get behind in studies because of poor schools abroad or alienation from teachers and peers upon his return could result in a failure that would affect the future status and security of the whole family. So this executive continued to leave his family in Tokyo, visiting them one weekend every few months.

Someone who was willing to give up so much to ensure his son's chances for academic success could also tremble at the threat of an unfavorable school report that would dash years of concerted family effort. What extraordinary power a teacher holds in his hands when he can say, "Now I have something to write about you in the *naishinsho*." And no student or parent will ever know for sure what was in the report.

The *Asahi Shimbun* has vigorously pressed to have these reports made accessible to students and parents in order to prevent mistakes and abuses. The paper claimed that some schools even switch one student's points to another student if the school considers that it can "win distinction" by sending more students to a prestigious institution. But the sanctity of these reports has been staunchly defended by Nikkyoso, the teachers' union.

Betrayed Their Children for Good Reports

Takako Suzuki began a crusade four years ago to defend her son who had been the constant victim of a homeroom teacher. She claimed that the teacher had inflicted physical punishment on many of his students for eleven years.

Originally, Suzuki was supported in her efforts by many other parents in Tokyo, but this support evaporated when the parents became worried about the effect the protest would have on their children's grades and school reports. Lamented Suzuki, "They betrayed the good of their children for good grades."

Critical of the other parents, Suzuki said, "They have given up their right to rear their own children by asking teachers to discipline their children through corporal punishment. It's the parents who are ultimately responsible for their children and their safety."

Rather than subject her children to the violence and intimidation that appeared to be routine at the school, Suzuki began teaching them at home. "Corporal punishment is absolutely unnecessary in education," she said. "Children must be taught by words no matter how many times the words have to be repeated" (Toshiya

Kawahara, "Corporal Punishment in Schools Illegal, But Cases of Battered Pupils on the Rise," *Japan Times*, 4-28-86).

The physical side of corporal punishment is only the most noticeable form of education brutality. Words themselves can often be even more damaging.

Battered by Words

Far more pervasive than physical violence is the verbal abuse that seriously affects young people at a vulnerable age in their lives. Words leave no visible scars and no hospital reports to be investigated. The evidence is nothing more than one person's word against another's. Concerned about this, Professor Minoru Yamamoto, from the educational department of Iwate University, has examined the issue in his book, *Education Reform from the Children's Viewpoint.*

Yamamoto surveyed 5,000 students on the matter of verbal attacks in the classroom. He even went to students' homes and collected the responses in sealed envelopes in order to ensure confidentiality.

In compiling the results, Yamamoto found that the teachers' viscious verbal attacks had caused serious emotional suffering. The unavoidable conclusion of the survey, according to Yamamoto, was that many teachers were abrasive adults who were bent on tormenting children.

"Children are clearly being judged on what grades they can make, not who they are," said Yamamoto. Indeed, "many of the teachers' abusive comments pertained to their students' intelligence or lack of it."

Examples of teachers' remarks that were reported by students:

"I advise you to take out a life insurance policy—an imbecile like you is better off dead."

"Your presence is a total discredit to society and school."

"Stupidity is said to be hereditary, and you sure took after your parents."

"Once a failure, always a failure."

"You are hopeless through and through."

"You belong in a kindergarten, not in this school."

In commenting on this study, education critic Michiko Nagahata said, "I was appalled by the deliberate cruelty with which some teachers rubbed salt into children's wounds. What caring parent or educator would ever harp maliciously on a youngster's failure or lack of physical beauty?

"Physical abuse leaves scars," continued Nagahata, "but verbal abuse can destroy a child internally. The only relief I felt was that this book was planned by teachers themselves."

The book was published by two prominent teachers' unions in northeast Japan but not without some hesitation. The critical portrayal of teachers in the classroom was worrisome because of concerns about public reaction.

"But we had to go ahead," said Masahiko Yamashita, deputy secretary-general of the Iwate prefectural high school teachers' union. "School education is in dire need of reform, but teachers are not always honest in admitting that problems must be addressed.

"Very often teachers feel obliged to cover up their colleagues' mistakes," continued Yamashita. "That, of course, doesn't win them the trust of concerned parents. I hope this book will serve as a new opportunity for parents and teachers to discuss their mutual problems as honestly as they can" (Noriyuki Nakatsuka, "Verbal Abuse from the Teacher," *Asahi Evening News*, 12-12-85).

Group Cover-up

Teachers who are disinclined to be open about disciplinary practices in the school frequently protect themselves and ensure a cover-up for each other by conducting their activities in groups.

A friend of mine, a teacher at a high school in Hokkaido, told me of a time when another teacher saw some students smoking. The man caught a few of the boys before they could run away and pulled them into a room.

Instead of attacking on his own, the teacher gathered a couple of other teachers into the room and locked the door. Thus mutually protected, they began to kick and hit the students in the stomach, trying to get them to reveal the names of those who got away. The boys were seriously hurt.

"An anonymous letter was sent to the newspaper about the incident, and a reporter was sent over to ask questions," commented my friend. "The principal and teachers denied everything.

"The newspaper didn't have anything more to go on, so they dropped the investigation. Secretly the teachers had their salaries reduced for a month or two.

"The coach is really mean. So are a few of the others. They beat kids all the time and everybody here knows it. But no one dares challenge the coach.

"Not too long ago he kicked two or three teeth out from one of our students. Because the parents complained, he had his salary docked 10 percent for three months. Still, the penalty is so light it isn't likely to change his attitude. And it doesn't compensate the victims. So what was the use?"

I did not have to ask him why he, himself, remained silent. I knew this man's dilemma and personality well enough. He had to spend his whole lifetime career in this school and in this town. He wasn't going to make everything miserable for himself through a brash confrontation with his coworkers. Besides, most of the teachers seemed to go along with it. He would tell me, a foreigner, about it instead, perhaps hoping that I could do something.

"The beatings are common . . . the salary reductions aren't," continued my friend. "Administrative penalties like that only happen if the principal finds that the incident has become a potential embarrassment to the school. The principals don't even want the police to know if a student hit a teacher because that implies to the authorities that we can't control our own students."

"Can't the reporters and police do more to investigate these complaints?" I asked.

"You don't know the power of these schools, both public and private. The men at the top are the pillars of the community and have tremendous influence with both the press and the police.

"Awhile back, a thirty-year-old clerk at the school committed suicide. It created quite a sensation internally. But that was hushed up, too. Really hushed up.

"The police never investigated and it never appeared in the news. We heard that there was a suicide note, but even that had been kept a mystery. As far as I know, only two people had a chance to see it. . . ."

Shroud of Secrecy

On another occasion I asked a professor if there had been any deaths among the several national universities in Hokkaido Prefecture where he taught. He remarked that there had been four deaths so far in the first six months of the year, a rather typical year for the combined student body of 5,000.

Naively, I probed, "How did the students at the university react to those deaths?"

"They don't know about them," replied the professor.

"But, surely the students must have read about it in the newspapers."

"It wasn't in the papers," he said. "Few people outside the school know anything about it."

"Why not?"

"The school officials feel that it would trouble the students unnecessarily. They have enough worries at this time in their lives, and students shouldn't have to start worrying about this kind of thing as well." It was clear from the conversation, however, that student sensitivities were not the only concerns of the teachers.

One superb reporter for the *Asahi Journal*, Yoshio Murakami, was able to penetrate this shroud of secrecy that usually envelops the educational labyrinth by listening to the complaints of parents at a school meeting. According to one account, a second year girl at a junior high school was called into the principal's office where five teachers were waiting for her.

Suddenly the beating began, reported Murakami. As the girl staggered, one of the teachers grabbed her by the hair and dragged her around the room. Her mother said that she almost fainted when her daughter returned home with a swollen face and terror-stricken eyes. But what recourse could this girl and her mother have against a whole group of such revered citizens?

On another occasion, a mother tried to criticize corporal punishment in a primary school meeting, Murakami reports. Suddenly there was applause in the room when the homeroom teacher cut her off saying, "You have to strike while the iron is hot. Beating them can instill a strong will in them." Another chimed in, "That's right. Mete out severe punishment" ("Corporal Punishment in Schools," *Asahi Evening News*, 9-21-85).

Just before Christmas in 1985, a twenty-seven-year-old teacher at a junior high school in Sagamihara, Kanagawa Prefecture, called a thirteen-year-old student into the faculty offices to ask if he had smoked cigarettes the previous day. Faculty desks were all arranged in neat rows across a large open room. This permitted all the other teachers to hear what was happening.

The boy refused to admit to smoking, so he was beaten around the head by the teacher. Before long, three other teachers joined the assailant in striking the boy ("Severe Corporal Punishment Assailed," *Japan Times*, 2-18-86).

One concerned foreign teacher explained to me that the girls at her school must bow in silence, with the teacher leaning back in his chair like a high priest sitting in judgment. "The kids have to be submissive and full of remorse, while being scolded or else they risk a renewed barrage of insults. Frequently the scolding continues until they are reduced to tears and all the signs of defiance are gone. They're literally broken."

She also explained to me that teachers place a lot of guilt onto the children. For example, teachers often tell students that they "broke a contract" when they violated a rule, thus evoking a sense of guilt in students who, of course, never had any part in making a contract.

The youths are yet unaware that voluntary, informed consent is the essential ingredient in any contractual arrangement. Surely the teacher would expect those ingredients in any contract into which he or she would enter.

Best and Worst

In a survey of 393 reported cases of corporal punishment in 1984, involving 2,433 students, it was revealed that 70 percent of the students received injuries and one student died. The fatality occurred when a student was forced to practice under harsh conditions following his request to quit an after-school rugby club. In another case of punishment, a teacher suspended a student upside down from a second floor window of the school.

Thirty-six percent of the students in these cases were female, 50 percent were from junior high schools, 31 percent from elementary school, and only 19 percent from high schools. Despite the expectation that older students would be more rebellious, the number of cases of corporal punishment dropped off dramatically in high school when youths were no longer compelled to attend.

Among the 488 teachers who gave out corporal punishment, only 8 percent were female, 114 were aged twenty-five to twenty-nine, and 122 taught physical education. Seventy-two percent of the teachers involved in the study, ones who were already exposed to public scrutiny, were given administrative punishments and 25 percent were fined for violating the criminal code.

Failure to do homework was the major reason for such punishment in the elementary grades, at 24 percent, while junior and senior high teachers indicated that students were punished for violations of school regulations and "teasing teachers" ("Most Students Who Received Corporal Punishment Got Hurt," *Asahi Evening News*, 12-9-85).

Fascinated by the idea of students "teasing their teachers," I questioned my student respondents about reports of students hitting teachers. Thirty-eight percent of the students in my survey group in Hakodate had seen students do just that.

Curious about their evaluation of the teachers they had, I asked the students what percentage of their teachers were excellent, good, all right, bad, or very bad. It surprised me to learn that these students had a generally low opinion of their mentors.

Excellent	10 percent
Good	14 percent
All right	33 percent
Bad	21 percent
Very bad	22 percent

Why was your worst teacher the worst?

was very selfish

never corrected her mistakes

lacked a human touch

was irritable

was stubborn

was always scolding

was very violent

couldn't or wouldn't understand feelings

was sly and sneaky, cunning

was moody and took everything out on the students

strange, like a robot

always wanted to be liked by every student

valued merit above effort

Why was your best teacher the best?

was understanding

made an effort to understand

was generous

was easy to understand

was frank

was tolerant

was a man of culture

told her view of life

generous in judgment and told many jokes

taught with all his heart

was concerned about his students, was friendly

was a refreshing teacher

gave parental advice

believed and cared for the students

loved us

It is easy to associate the first set of descriptions with corporal punishment and quite difficult to picture a teacher in the latter group using corporal punishment. This, too, is a matter of some debate in Japan. Just how much love is expressed with corporal punishment, referred to commonly as the "whip of love"?

7

THE WHIP OF LOVE

To me, teachers today seem to be doing their best to be disliked by their pupils.

—Tomiji Hasegawa

An English conversation teacher in Kushiro City, Kochi Harada, declared, "Corporal punishment does not represent the love of the teacher. The moment the teacher strikes his pupil, he becomes lower than the student and no longer remains the 'teacher.' Love is not conveyed through corporal punishment, but through the sincerity of the teacher. Schools as well as teachers should immediately think of a nonviolent method of pupil guidance."

Harada described a conversation with a new teacher who said that his senior colleagues advised him to hit the students regularly in order to get the students to obey and to maintain their respect. "I was taken aback to know that such an atmosphere prevailed over the school, and that the headmaster tolerates such acts by the teachers. After learning of the situation, I could not help but think that the cause of school violence and bullying lies greatly in the teachers themselves.

"Having been a teacher in the past, I must also confess that more than a couple of times I hit my pupils. I now regret doing so, and painfully remember my deeds," concluded Harada ("Heavy Hand of Love," *Asahi Evening News*, 12-5-85).

This view was complemented by that of a housewife in Kagamihara City, Gifu Prefecture. Sumie Kamiya asserted, "Since bullying among children has become a large social problem, what about the teachers' hidden bullying of children under the name of corporal punishment?"

Corporal punishment is "actually conducted by teachers on their pupils at schools—seemingly the safest place—with the most reliable teachers. When the children forgot to bring something from home, didn't eat all their lunch or broke some rules, they were given lynch-like punishment in front of their classmates such as being made to take off their underwear or punched until medical treatment was necessary or locked up in lockers" ("Corporal Punishment is Bullying," *Asahi Evening News*, 11-4-85).

A student at the Tokyo symposium on violence in the schools testified that his gym teacher snubbed him for months despite repeated attempts to apologize for some infraction of the rules. "The only times she let me get close to her to speak were when nobody else was looking so she could kick me hard," said the youth.

"When she finally accepted my apology, she glared at me and hissed, 'Do it once again and you'll never reach home alive.' She used to tell the class that she beat us because she cared."

"For Their Own Good"

One prefectural school board official at the symposium said that "society tends to glorify 'hot-blooded' teachers who resort to physical means in trying to keep disobedient and rebellious students in line . . . and meaness is too often taken for zeal." He continued, "More teachers than I care to think about overrate corporal punishment as the best and most effective means of educating the unruly young" (Masaru Nishigaito, "Violence at the Teachers' Hands," *Asahi Evening News*, 11-27-85).

Not only was this rationale offered by most of the teachers that I talked to, even in defiance of their own union's public stand against corporal punishment, but it was also often espoused by the young people themselves. At Giyo High School, where Toshinao Takahashi was beaten to death by his teacher, 40 percent of the students in one class expressed that they were in favor of corporal punishment saying, "It can't be helped."

About half the students in my own surveys asserted that the blows they received were for their own good. This is surely a testament to the effectiveness of any indoctrination—when the victims of abuse sanction the actions of their tormentors.

The National Education Research Institute claimed that 46 percent of the teachers support corporal punishment as a means of discipline. This was in spite of the fact that more than 60 percent of the teachers believed that such punishment could not bring positive educational results, violated human rights of children, and harmed the teacher-student relationships ("Almost Half of Teachers Polled Support Corporal Punishment," *Asahi Evening News*, 3-12-86).

I believe the real percentages of support and acquiescence to be much higher than the official statistics reveal. Of all the teachers and teachers-in-training with whom I have discussed this issue, even some of the kindest and gentlest among them agreed on the necessity of hitting students.

Sweet Harue Watanabe giggled when I asked her about corporal punishment at the private junior high school for girls where she was a music teacher. She was a thoroughly beautiful person who was well read in the classics, had a lovely family, and enjoyed a rich appreciation of delicate poetry.

Her face turned red, and she shrank in embarrassment at my question. Sheepishly she replied, in a voice that was barely audible, "I sometimes hit my students."

There was no doubt in my mind that she really did love her students and that her "blows" could not have been physically damaging to anyone. So, then, why not words instead of slaps? Which did she want her students to imitate as they grew up? Whose pattern of behavior was she following?

As gentle, as soft-hearted, and as timid as Watanabe was, I could not imagine her originating the idea of such violence. Nor could I picture her defending a student against the more vicious *taibatsu* of a school coach.

"To Make Them Like Me"

One zealous practitioner of physical punishment was Tomiji Hasegawa, a retired English teacher and coach who worked at a junior high school in Mito City for thirty-four years after the war. "Firstly, to make my students good at English," recounted Hasegawa, "I tried to make them like the language. To this end, I tried to make them like me because students naturally do not study a subject diligently if they don't like the teacher.

"To make myself liked, I abolished all uniforms for both the students as well as for myself. In the past, junior high schools were open-minded in such respects. Three-quarters of my class was taught seriously but attractively, while the remaining one-fourth consisted of lectures about my true feelings and past experiences.

"I administered corporal punishment to those who were noisy during classes, despised the physical handicaps of others or their parents' professions, bullied weaker students, or blackmailed other students and stole things. But my preaching never went beyond three minutes. Both the children as well as their parents understood my intentions whenever I hit them for their misconduct.

"As for the baseball team," continued Hasegawa, "there were almost no holidays for the team members throughout the year. But they were free to quit whenever they wanted to. Since my hair was long, the team members were also free to choose their hair style. When they made stupid errors or didn't play seriously during a match, I hit them regardless of victory or loss. It was surprising that as the team grew stronger and began to win matches, the members didn't mind being hit. It should also be noted that their schoolwork results improved. . . .

"To me," concluded Hasegawa, "teachers today seem to be doing their best to be disliked by their pupils" (Tomiji Hasegawa, "How to Make Friends," *Asahi Evening News*, 2-13-86).

Constitutional Issues

Hasegawa reflects the attitude of many teachers who expect their intentions to speak louder than their actions. Of course, one wonders if he, too, might have stopped hitting his students if he had had regard for students' intentions rather than their actions and supposed errors.

Hasegawa, an English teacher, knew exactly what he was saying when he stated that he tried to "make" the students good at English, to "make" them like the language, and to "make" them like him. These imperatives diminish the virtue of the end result.

In order "to make myself liked," Hasegawa felt that it was necessary to abolish the requirement of uniforms for the students and for himself. This raises a crucial point: the difference between privileges and rights, between subjects and human beings.

Privileges come into existence when rulers, of any kind, temporarily suspend onerous rules that subjects were previously obliged to obey. Subjects would then be expected to show their gratitude to the ruler by liking him . . . so long as the favors or privileges were continued.

Rights, on the other hand, belong to all human beings. Rulers may decide to help protect these rights or they may try to interfere with them, but human beings are not obliged to be grateful to a ruler who has chosen to respect these rights. Any ruler who promises not to interfere with rights in order to be liked is exercising intimidation, not justice.

This is precisely the issue, or problem of definition, which underlies the philosophical confrontation in Japan today. On the one side is the Japan Bar Association, the media, some educators, students, and parents who argue for greater respect of children's rights. And on the other side are the courts, many administrators, educators, parents, and even students who argue that young people earn privileges from society as a whole by being obedient.

In siding with this latter group the courts ruled emphatically, in November 1985, that there was no basis for the claim that a school rule mandating short haircuts for boys violated basic human rights.

The Kumamoto District Court in southeastern Japan stated that, while the rule cannot be shown to have any positive effect on education, there is nothing unconstitutional about it.

The parents of 17-year-old Kenichiro Shino asked the court for compensation amounting to ¥100,000 (about $450 at the time) for the mental anguish that the boy suffered as a result of the regulations. School regulations mandated a closely-cropped cut while Kenichiro kept his hair long.

After the school principal scolded Kenichiro, he became the target of bullying by his classmates. This reached such intensity that he was finally forced to stay home from school for two weeks.

The court decision contained these points: (1) There is no indication of a social consensus on whether the close-cropped hairstyle is appropriate for today's junior high students; (2) Hygiene cannot be cited as justification for the rule; (3) There is no evidence that keeping students' hair short prevents delinquency.

"Although the hairstyle regulations are considered to have little to do with educational purposes, there can be found no unreasonableness in allowing school authorities to use their discretion concerning such regulations," said presiding Judge Shigeo Tsuchiya. In addition, Judge Tsuchiya dismissed an appeal since Kenichiro had already graduated and was therefore no longer subject to the regulations ("Hairstyle Regulations Constitutional: Court," *Daily Yomiuri*, 11-14-85).

Both sides of the court battle believed that this verdict would have far reaching consequences. The defendants worried that an adverse ruling would throw doubt on all school rules. The plaintiffs worried that this judgment would put the official stamp of approval on any and all regulations (Charles M. De Wolf, "The Haircut Verdict: Lessons to Be Learned," *Asahi Evening News*, 11-29-85).

Just four months later, the principal and homeroom teachers at Onomichi Municipal Nagae Primary School in Hiroshima grabbed up scissors and clipped the hair of all 53 sixth-grade boys just before graduation. Toshiya Nitta, the principal, told reporters that the action was not forced by a school rule but was merely recommended. Whether the rule was written or unwritten, overt or covert, the courts guaranteed that the power was to remain intact ("Now That's What I Call a Haircut," *Asahi Evening News*, 2-27-86).

Considerable publicity has been given to one brave student's family that challenged the *marugari* regulations that still mandate hairstyles in a third of the nation's junior high schools. In 1987, Tadashi Moriyama went to Aoi Junior High School in Okazaki city with hair that was six centimeters longer than the mandatory 0.9 cm. His teachers kept him after school, telling him that he had to cut his hair or else the older students would deal with him.

Hearing of this, Tadashi's father, Akio warned the school of court action if the harassment continued. This didn't stop the student bullies who persisted in bullying the boy in the halls, until the *Asahi Shimbun* [one of Japan's largest newspapers] took up the cause and began to run a series of articles about the case. Tadashi became a celebrity to the media, and the harassment stopped at school. But then the Moriyama family received dozens of threatening calls at home. Some callers warned, "Get out of Okazaki or something will happen to you."

A survey found that three-quarters of the students opposed the *marugari* rule, but this made little impact on the principal and those teachers who were bent on perpetuating it as a rite of passage. "But the schools are not entirely to blame," declared Aoki Moriyama, founder of the budding anti-*marugari* movement. "This situation could not exist without the parents' support" (Christian Huggett, "Okazaki Boy Struggles for Independence from School's Close-Cropped Conformity," *Japan Times*, 2-27-90).

If one were to view the Japanese schoolyard as a training ground for democracy, then democracy is in jeopardy. For the students learn by such examples that their condition is governed not by rights, but by powers beyond their reach, by the whim of autocratic rulers, and by the discouragement of independent thought and action.

Free to Choose?

"Since my hair was long," declared Hasegawa, "the team members were also free to choose their hairstyle." At least Hasegawa

was not hypocritical like so many of his colleagues who have
insisted on having hairstyles that were denied to the students. Still,
Hasegawa was wrong in saying that the students were free to
choose, because the students' choice was first dependent on the
choice of Hasegawa's own hairstyle and his permission to allow
them to do the same.

Did the same logic hold for every other rule concerning apparel
and behavior as well? If Hasegawa smoked, and the odds being
very high among Japanese men, he probably did, then would the
students also be allowed to smoke?

Indeed, the high incidence of smoking among adult Japanese
men indicates that youngsters in Japan developed far more of their
life-long traits from imitating their elders than from the artificiality
of the rules in school.

Lastly, it is noteworthy that Hasegawa mentions that students
were free to quit his baseball team whenever they wanted to,
although it is possible that the pressures of *naishinsho* prevented
them from doing so. And Hasegawa neglects to mention that the
students were not free to quit his English class, and the populace
was not free to quit paying his salary whenever they wanted to.

In a land of Buddha, where violence is abhorred by many, there
were undoubtedly some people who might have preferred not to
pay Hasegawa's salary, objecting to corporal punishment on ethical grounds, legal grounds, practical educational grounds, or any
combination of the three. Nevertheless, they were forced to give
him money. Was there, then, any hypocrisy in Hasegawa's punishment of students who may have used intimidation or force to take
money from classmates?

Students in my class at the teachers' college were asked whether
or not they agreed with the following statement: "When a student
has a bad teacher, the student and parents should be able to choose
a new teacher."

Agree   15

Disagree   1

Abstain   1

Explanations:

We don't have to give up expressing our opinions.

It's unfair to have a bad teacher.

We don't have to be the victim of bad teachers.

We have a right to study so we should be able to enjoy our school life.

We spend most of the day with the teacher, so we have the right to choose teachers.

Because we go to school to study we want to choose a good teacher.

Students are affected by bad teachers, and they don't have to stand for it.

The student learns not from class but from personality.

There are many new good teachers who could teach.

Every student has a right to a good education.

Children should have a good environment.

It doesn't solve the problem because other students still have a bad teacher.

Bad relations exist and are unavoidable.

A bad teacher is a good experience.

Then they were asked to respond to this statement: "I have a right not to pay for a bad teacher."

Agree	1
Disagree	11
Abstain	4

They did not believe that people had the right to refuse to pay a bad teacher. The conversation turned on the hardship that such a practice would bring to the teacher, albeit a bad teacher. And what about the consequences to the student that must suffer a bad teacher? In a comparison of the suffering of students with the suffering of an unemployed teacher, the students usually lost.

So things will remain the same, always difficult to replace bad teachers with good teachers. And the struggle of avoiding bad teachers will continue to be the lonely struggle of each new student and each new set of parents looking for a way out.

Theorists have long been intrigued by the Japanese ability to accept ambiguity and contradiction. Some say that this is not exclusive to Japan, but in postwar Japan this trait is more obvious because the Japanese have had so many Western regulations superimposed on their culture.

For example, constitutional provisions exist to prohibit monopolies and a military while the actual policies of government actively promote monopolies and the military on a grand scale. I do not wish to single out the Japanese for this slight-of-hand behavior. Every nationality has been just as capable of such contradictions. My Japanese friends were quick to point out that Americans, for instance, have always been thoroughly capable of reconciling the military draft with constitutional prohibitions against involuntary servitude.

While visiting in Tokyo one summer, I pressed an acquaintance for an explanation to the "Tanaka Puzzle." Kakuei Tanaka was the former prime minister who had been forced to resign as leader of the Liberal Democratic Party (LDP) due to the 1973 Lockheed bribery scandal. Nevertheless, despite all the exposure of corruption, Tanaka remained king-maker of Japanese politics for another thirteen years.

This was the puzzle: "How is it that Tanaka, a convicted criminal with nothing more than an elementary school education, became the most powerful man in a nation that preaches the utmost obedience to law and the supreme value of education to the success of all the children?"

The reply was a shrug of the shoulders and the Japanese tilt—a tip of the head to the right, accompanied by the audible sound of air being sucked through the teeth. Then, "That's politics." Until there is a better answer to that puzzle, it seems that the proper education of the young will also remain an unsolved riddle.

The Master of Ceremonies

In the Hakodate civic center, the local PTA held a meeting in which one speaker after another rose to tell the audience about the evils of *ijime* (student bullying) and what parents could do to understand it and combat it. First it was the education specialist Shooji Teraoka, then the chief of Hakodate's reformatory.

The Master of Ceremonies seemed to be a very distinguished, concerned man, Takemichi Hosaka. Hosaka was introduced as the man in charge of the PTA's *Ijime* Awareness Program. A friend of mine, who knew of my interest in corporal punishment, leaned over and whispered allegations about Hosaka's background.

"Hosaka *sensei* [teacher] is also the most famous for hitting students. He was even called in to the city office and scolded for it. But it didn't stop him. He told them, 'I don't care if I'm fired. I want to make my students good.' "

My informant continued, "Hosaka gained his reputation as a strict teacher by calming a very violent school, Tokura Junior High. Now, at his new post at Fukabori, a school of 950 students, the atmosphere isn't as good. Some of the parents are against sending their kids to Fukabori. Now Hosaka is feared by students, and, at the same time, he is famous for his concern about *ijime*."

It seemed worthwhile to interview this famous man. Was he the *ijime/taibatsu* contradiction incarnate? Or was he really a mild mannered guardian of the youth? So I asked around and found a woman who agreed to arrange an interview.

When I arrived at Fukabori Junior High School, I found Hosaka to be cordial, yet stern. He was dressed in a modest black sweater and white shirt. And while we talked, he usually gazed past me out the window.

"Some schools have 200 to 300 rules," he said. "This school probably has the least number . . . perhaps 15, with sub-categories. Fewer rules are better. The school never controls what a student thinks. If they did, then it would be just the same as Russia. Here, we try to respect individuality. . . .

"The teachers' load at the school is very heavy and increasing. Sometimes a teacher has 140 students. For every month, week, day, the school makes a detailed curriculum guide for all academic subjects. We even use this as a guide in building personality by giving a study of ethics. This is necessary to prevent delinquency. . . .

"The Ministry of Education gives out a booklet entitled *The Limits of Freedom*, which helps people to understand that there must not be too much freedom," said Hosaka. "Most people misunderstand freedom . . . it is viewed as a kind of selfishness. . . .

"One of the problems we have to deal with here is that of pregnancy in the girls, as young as 15. There is a sex education book that is published to help the teachers to deal with this. For example, it teaches the importance of purity of mind and body. . . .

"The traditional way is to say that purity is a good point in a woman, and they should be more shy in talking about sex. Nowadays, the good way is to be more open. Boys are more childish and there is no problem about sex education. . . .

"Women, too, are now more open. They have been changed a great deal by women's liberation. Many of them have jobs, a kind of individual expression. . . .

"However, we should think about a woman's special character, that is, to become a mother. The most important thing is her discipline. For example, a woman should be feminine and it is through education that she can be encouraged toward consideration, kindness, warmth, and neatness. . . ."

"Education has developed much since the war. Now the emphasis is on how to raise children and how to make quality. . . ."

I inquired, "Do the students like the rules here?"

"I don't think so," replied Hosaka. "But they, as a collective, think we need them."

"Can they recommend changes?"

"It is very complicated. The school board and the parents must consider everything in order to permit the changes. We give many methods of democracy, otherwise it would be like Marcos' dictatorship."

"Have they changed the rules at all?"

"Some schools say they don't have to wear the cap, others can alter the uniform."

"What kinds of *ijime* go on here?"

"Sometimes ten students will attack one. Sometimes it's physical or threats or just ostracization. The examinations are intense, and the strong sometimes would just eat the weak."

"What kinds of regulations are there for the teachers' clothing?"

"No regulations," said Hosaka. "That's left up to common sense."

"Are teachers very interested in the union here?"

"Only three of the forty teachers belong to the union."

"Is there bullying among teachers?" I asked.

"Teachers sometimes bully other teachers who come from different universities or districts. It is very difficult to go to the top and become an executive in a position to control others if one is not from the dominant school in the area. In Hakodate, that would be Hokkaido University."

"Is there racial discrimination in the schools?" I inquired.

"Some districts have prejudice. For example, the Ainu, Koreans, and Filipinos have their own Japanese schools."

"How about *taibatsu*?"

"Corporal punishment is most often practiced by the young teachers who are inexperienced and have no method for teaching. Hitting is a very delicate problem, and it isn't good if it is done emotionally or like bullying. Some teachers do it in a way that is good. For instance, some parents ask the teacher to hit the children. Teachers who are worried about a child, yet cannot make him or her good, give a kind of whip of love."

"Then, do the young imitate those teachers?"

"Well, the quality is different," responded Hosaka. "It's not the same kind of punishment. Corporal punishment is against the law so I don't think we should do it, but some teachers feel that a child is like his own child and sometimes the teacher will treat the child like the child is sick. Corporal punishment might be permitted under those circumstances."

"Does the law allow for these exceptions?"

"I think so. One student who disturbs the class can be made to stand all through the class. But all students have the right to attend the class. A student with problems never changes his classes, but he can change schools."

"What happens if a student doesn't go to school because of corporal punishment?"

"I never saw an example where a student refused to go to school due to corporal punishment. The base of education, after all, is kindness and gentleness."

8

MAY HIS SOUL SLEEP IN PEACE

I don't want to die, but it's like living in hell to go on like this.
—Hirofumi Shikagawa

Two weeks before a judgment was handed down in the trial of Amamori, the teacher who killed a student over the use of a hair dryer, another death shook the nation. This time lawsuits began to fly, politicians called for investigations, school officials were fired, and students were charged with crimes.

These extraordinary measures were being taken in a country where authority is seldom questioned and where problems are more commonly swept under the carpet. Some politicians and parents were finally demanding that the education hierarchy itself should shoulder the blame for the horrendous behavior of teachers and administrators.

It all started as a fairly simple case of schoolyard intimidation, which mushroomed into a morbid nightmare for Hirofumi Shikagawa. Shikagawa was a thirteen-year-old, second-year student at Nakano Fujimi Junior High School near Tokyo.

He was quiet, short at just over five feet, and had a bushy head of black hair, which was parted down the center. His baby face and slight frame made Shikagawa an easy mark for those youths and adults who were bent on tormenting him.

The bullying began in June 1985 when a group of students formed a musical band and enlisted young Shikagawa to play the drums. Shikagawa found a sense of belonging with this group, even though the others occasionally teased him. Gradually, he became a little servant for them, carrying their school bags and running errands.

Shikagawa usually served as the courier between his group and a rival band, which was composed of older, third-year students. After the two bands practiced a few times together in the fall, they decided to combine into a single group.

A Mock Funeral

About this time, in October, Shikagawa's situation took a turn for the worse. The band leaders had rented a studio in town for night practices, and Shikagawa's father would not let him stay out late. So the older students made fun of him and began to pester him at school.

Band members went into Shikagawa's classroom and used a felt-tipped pen to paint a moustache over his mouth and circles around his eyes. They even forced him to sing songs out on the schoolyard and to do little jigs in the hallways.

In mid-November, forty of Shikagawa's peers conducted a mock funeral for him—complete with burning incense and flowers covering his desk. The students prepared the traditional square of paper, a condolence card, which contained the signatures of all his classmates and, surprisingly, four of his teachers.

The homeroom teacher, fifty-seven-year-old Namio Fujisaki, bid farewell to Shikagawa, writing, "May his soul sleep in peace." Other teachers signed off saying, "Take care of yourself, good-bye," and "Rest in peace."

Shikagawa was devastated by this collective ridicule. Because everyone, students and teachers alike, collaborated against him, he did everything to avoid school. All together, he missed twenty-seven days of class.

Sometimes he would complain of headaches or stomach pains so that he could stay home. On days that he did go to school Shikagawa spent more and more of his time hiding in the boys' restroom in order to escape the embarrassment that awaited him in class.

On a few occasions he would take the train to Iwate Prefecture to visit his grandmother. She was the only one who could give him genuine, although temporary, refuge.

"I'm Going to Kill Shikagawa"

When Shikagawa finally did show up at school again, several boys picked fights with him and sent him home battered and bloody. On a couple of occasions, his father called the school authorities for an explanation and every time he was assured that everything possible was being done to protect his son.

"Perhaps," the father was told, "you should find another school for your boy." But moving to another school, where he would be a newcomer and outsider, only increased the likelihood that he would face more bullying in the future.

Unsatisfied with the lack of protection at the school, Shikagawa's mother filed a complaint with the local police. She protested that her son had every right to be safe from this continuous violence. However, the police did not take the matter seriously, and no action was taken.

So, his father tried again. This time he complained directly to the parents of the bullies. Ironically, there were repercussions that made life worse for his son. On the day following the father's call on the mother of one of the attackers, the Shikagawa household received anonymous phone calls threatening their son's life.

Can't Refuse the Group

According to one senior high school teacher in Tokyo, Haruko Murata, many young people are too weak to break away from groups of peers that abuse them. "Fearing possible loss of contact with the group, the bullied child never retaliates. Instead," observed Murata, "he continues to stay close to the group because he would feel uneasy away from them."

While many young people become resigned to their poor treatment, young Shikagawa was not so timid. Having tolerated this swinging band of bullies long enough, he tried to break away and start new friendships. On the last day of the year, Shikagawa joined another group of classmates who went on a sunrise hike to the top of Takao, a mountain north of Tokyo.

Unfortunately, the old gang was not going to let Shikagawa go. On his first day back at school, all the members surrounded him and beat him severely.

The next six school days Shikagawa left home, but he never showed up for class. Again, he hid out around town and never told his parents where he was going. But this, too, could get him into trouble if he was discovered by the police and reported to the school authorities. A record of truancy could ruin his future.

One last time, in desperation, he returned to school hoping that the other students would have finally forgotten about tormenting him and would ease up a bit. It was futile. As soon as he was spotted, Shikagawa was forced to climb to the top of a tree and sing. And, just as before, the teachers were either helpless or they were in league with the bullies.

Shikagawa finally stopped going to school entirely. An outcast and in misery, he traveled to northern Japan to see his grandmother one more time. She was not home. Later, in anguish, his grandmother sobbed, "I'm sure he came up here to see me, and if I hadn't been out at the time, he might be alive now" ("Bullied Suicide Victim Eulogized in Rites," *Japan Times*, 2-4-86).

At last, young Shikagawa tore a scrap of paper from a shopping bag and addressed a note to his family and friends. "I don't want to die, but it's like living in hell to go on like this." He named two students who had tyrannized him at school and pleaded with them to stop bullying anyone else. His body was found later that night, hanging from a coat hook on a toilet door in Morioka train station.

Shikagawa's death was, indeed, tragic. But the Japanese are not unaccustomed to suicides among young people, and this case might have passed as all the others, without a ripple of public outcry, if it had not been for the unusually candid investigation into his death.

The Investigation

Police officials, embarrassed by press disclosures that Shikagawa's mother had received no help from the local police, were intent on correcting this error and in clearing themselves by finding other culprits. Thus, the Metropolitan Police Department sent seven investigators to conduct the local inquiry.

Furthermore, the Tokyo District Public Prosecutor's Office prepared charges against several students who were accused of assaulting the victim. In Japan, such a charge is tantamount to conviction since judges rarely ever rule against the Public Prosecutor.

The school's principal, Isao Nishikawa, cancelled classes for a few days and called all of the students into an emergency convocation where he admonished them to put an end to the kind of intimidation that had led to Shikagawa's death. In response to questioning by the police and by reporters, Nishikawa calmly explained that the school had done everything that it could for the unfortunate boy.

Nishikawa offered assurances that the school had followed up on complaints that Shikagawa's father had made a couple months before. He claimed that the students involved in the bullying had been counseled and that they had promised their cooperation.

The Cover-up

Then, less than a week after the suicide, the wall of secrecy broke, and the public learned that four teachers had participated in the mock funeral for Shikagawa. Worse still, the teachers had tried to enlist the aid of students in covering up.

Shikagawa's homeroom teacher, Fujisaki, became fearful for his job and asked the students to keep quiet about his participation in the eulogies. Some of the students took advantage of the teacher's embarrassment and vulnerability to increase their bullying activity. Eventually, the whole story was leaked to the press.

Once on the scent, investigators probed Fujisaki's background and character. In no time at all the police found even more justification for disciplinary action against him. Fujisaki, it was discovered, had been violating school regulations for over twenty-five years by moonlighting as a test maker at another school.

Shortly after the mock funeral was reported on the news, a flood of letters flowed into the Nakano Education Commission from parents who wanted to pull their children out of school. Even the parents of children at the affiliated elementary school began looking around for other schools.

More than a hundred parents poured into an impromptu Parent Teacher Association meeting to express their concern and to announce that they were watching developments closely. Having just resumed normal hours, classes were again cut back to short morning sessions throughout the week while the teachers held a long string of emergency meetings to discuss the lack of confidence that was brewing in the community.

It is not unusual for a faculty meeting to last anywhere from two to nine hours after the regular workday. Under these extraordinary conditions, the faculty faced intense pressure to shore up a crumbling school reputation that had personal and career implications for each and every one them. A connection with such a scandal could brand all of those working at the school for the rest of their lives.

"Go Kill Yourself!"

Before the storm could die down, another crisis struck. A potential murder and another suicide were narrowly averted and, this time, it gave the public a more than subtle clue to the sordid state inside the classroom.

On the day that the regular class schedule resumed, Manabu Saito, a twenty-nine-year-old science teacher who had participated in the mock funeral for Shikagawa, was being challenged in class by one of the bullies that Shikagawa had named in his suicide note. Saito told the bully to stop playing with a bottle of cologne, and the boy refused.

The young tough teased Saito by saying that the teacher was incapable of enforcing any discipline at all. To prove his point, the bully began beating on the student who was sitting in front of him. Other students later testified that the boy in front was hit thirty to forty times over a twenty-minute period.

"You are another Shikagawa," yelled the aggressor. "Kill yourself like Shikagawa." Finally, he came around the desk and pounded his prey several times in the face.

Throughout this onslaught, the victimized boy repeatedly cried out to the teacher for help. The teacher completely ignored this pleading until the boy turned to wrestle with his attacker. Then, unexpectedly, the teacher told the victim, not the attacker, to "Stop it!" ("Students Say Teacher Didn't Stop Beating," *Asahi Evening News*, 2-14-86).

At this, the victim ran from the room shouting that he would get a knife and kill the other boy and then he would commit suicide. Alarmed, the teacher ran after him and tried to prevent him from going into a hardware store for a knife.

This struggle in front of the hardware store attracted the attention of officials who were watching from a nearby police station. The police questioned both of them and learned just enough to realize that they needed to expand their whole investigation of the Shikagawa case.

They arrested the bully on suspicion of assault and filed a report that immediately caught the eye of reporters, who had little access to the school itself. Badgering the school principal for details, they insisted on a news conference. This conference was handled so clumsily by the principal that it eventually led to his dismissal.

The Second Cover-up

Sitting formally before the cameras that evening, Nishikawa, the principal, introduced Saito to the media and then allowed the teacher to explain everything in a manner that was designed to take the heat off the school. Saito claimed that he knew nothing of callous references to the Shikagawa suicide during class. Furthermore, Saito said that he scolded the bully several times that morning and that he put an immediate stop to violence after the bully had struck his victim a single blow.

This might have put the whole matter to rest except that the victim's mother, and several student witnesses, became incensed at the manner in which the incident had been distorted. The woman knew that her son had not come home upset and with a swollen face as the result of a single blow. So, she filed a protest with the school board. This led to another wave of investigations.

By now, the highest echelons of government were being drawn into the scrap. On the day of Saito's press conference one of the major opposition political parties, the Buddhism-oriented Komeito Party, urged Prime Minister Yasuhiro Nakasone to adopt a five-point educational reform proposal for the nation, which included immediate measures to deal with bullying in the schools. In response, the Education Ministry was prodded by Nakasone into summoning local school board officials for an explanation of the crisis—a crisis that was shaking confidence in districts across the country.

Making a public show of concern, the ruling Liberal Democratic Party (LDP) sent a committee on school bullying to Nakano Junior High for an impromptu inspection. Seven of the twenty-two committee members stayed at the school for a grand total of forty-five minutes. Fifteen minutes were spent at the school gate watching students arrive, and thirty minutes were spent in the principal's office listening to an explanation of why Shikagawa died.

Perhaps in anticipation of the LDP arrival, graffiti had been scrawled across the name plate of the school, adjacent to the gate where party officials would stand. It read, *Ninpinin*, telling the world that this institution was like a "heartless brute."

Throughout the Nakano District someone distributed leaflets and posters that identified, publicly for the first time, one of the bullies that Shikagawa wrote about in his suicide note. The flyers demanded that the bully and his mother be publicly disgraced.

"They have never visited the house of Shikagawa whom they killed," declared the anonymous author. "Let's get the demonic child and mother in front of the public, and let's not forgive what they did."

"Student Guidance"

Meanwhile, the newspapers were coming down hardest on the teachers. An editorial in the *Yomiuri Shimbun* (2-17-86), Japan's largest daily, shouted its judgment with the headline, "Teachers on Trial." Said the editors, "It is regrettable that the police had to be brought into the picture. School authorities and the teachers are to blame for ignoring the significance of Shikagawa's death."

The teachers felt obliged to defend themselves with a white paper that was distributed by Nikkyoso, the Japan Teachers' Union. While not specifically denying responsibilty for what goes on in the schools, the union survey attempted to excuse the teachers from responsibility by noting that they felt overwhelmed by the burdens of large class sizes, long working hours, and uncontrollable students.

Another survey, by the Japan Youth Research Institute (JYRI), was published within two weeks of Shikagawa's suicide. It found that 70 percent of the nation's teachers believed that home life was largely responsible for students' problems. Only a small minority of the teachers indicated that the schools should resolve the problems within and not foist the blame on others.

Since most teachers believed that the problems originated in the home, many felt that little or nothing could be done at school other than to contain the crisis. Thirty percent of the teachers polled said that *taibatsu* (physical punishment) was unavoidable as a means of "student guidance," particularly in the case of mammoth-sized schools with very large classes.

In order to determine whether the teachers were up to this kind of physical "student guidance" at the Nakano school, the head of the education board examined the sex and age of all the teachers at the school. He concluded that an imbalance in these factors had contributed to the lack of control.

The study found that there were no male teachers in the prime thirty-five to forty-five age bracket—such teachers are the ones who were deemed to have the experience and physical strength that were necessary for this kind of "student guidance." Therefore, officials at Nakano Junior High submitted a request to the education board for more teachers who could mete out physical punishment.

This was a difficult request to fulfill. Shizuo Arai, head of the education board, declared that there are very few male teachers in this age group and those who are of the right age do not usually want to transfer schools.

The irony in all of this is that Nakano Junior High was pushing to beef up corporal punishment while the court in Gifu Prefecture was busy chastising Giyo High for its overemphasis on corporal punishment. It was at Giyo High that Toshinao Takahashi had been killed the previous year.

Which, then, results in the death of students? Too much *taibatsu* or too little? Or does this question miss the point altogether? If *taibatsu* is designed to hold students reponsible for their bad behavior, then what will be done to hold teachers responsible for their bad behavior? And what incentives exist for good, constructive behavior?

Shikagawa's Final Message

The investigators at Nakano Junior High ultimately decided to punish those who were a party to the death of young Shikagawa. In an unprecedented step, the Tokyo Metropolitan Education Board took disciplinary action against the school principal and five teachers. The principal, Nishikawa, was forced to resign, and Fujisaki, Shikagawa's homeroom teacher, was dismissed in disgrace.

Another teacher who had participated in the mock funeral was also dismissed, and other teachers were reprimanded, suffered cuts in pay, or were ordered to attend one-year training sessions outside the school. In addition, the Tokyo Metropolitan Police Department arrested sixteen students at the school for a variety of violent crimes.

Most encouraging of all, Shikagawa's parents filed a pathbreaking ¥22 million ($170,000) damage suit against the Nakano Board of Education, the Tokyo Metropolitan Government, and the parents of two bullies who were named in the suicide note. In a letter of complaint, the Shikagawa family stated that the school overlooked the signs of bullying and, through the actions of the teachers, even contributed to their son's death. The parents said that they were not seeking compensation for the suicide death, rather they believed that this was the only way to make sure that effective measures were taken to prevent bullying in the future.

Many children have committed suicide in Japan, but subsequent legal action by the family is rare. One reason is that it is so difficult to prove the connection between bullying and a suicide. In this case, however, young Shikagawa may have done many other young people a great service by having written that last note and having given the names of those who pushed him to that tragic end.

Sadly, these steps toward a lawsuit seem to have turned the public against the Shikagawa family. As in the Takahashi case, the family itself has come under some ruthless scrutiny that raised questions about the stability of the family and the motives of the suit.

One acquaintance asked me if I had seen Shikagawa's parents on television. "They are kind of strange parents," he said. "It seems that they were at fault, too, and now they are using the point to their benefit. They hope to get a lot of money from their son's death."

And so, the blame continues to be passed. For some, it is a way to shift the responsibility onto the shoulders of others. Yet the debate itself may cause everyone to re-examine society's attitudes toward young people. Perhaps society should shoulder the blame for compelling youngsters like Shikagawa to suffer a learning environment that is unbearable.

Chameleon Schools

To Westerners, the perplexing discipline problem in Japan is a surprise because "the Japanese school" is so often depicted in television specials, books, and articles as the nearly perfect learning environment. "If that ideal image is true," I am so often asked by friends in the United States, "then how could students be so much out of control at times? And why would such great numbers of teachers believe that physical beatings are necessary to manage the daily lives of young people who are normally so obedient?"

My answer is that the school image is partly a facade. Foreign observers, journalists, and writers frequently overlook quirks in the system. One reason for this is that the Japanese are intensely concerned about what foreigners think about Japan. Therefore, the hospitality that foreigners are afforded is always superb. There is a certain chameleon-like transformation that occurs when outsiders arrive for visits.

Every student and staff and faculty member is aware of the mutual necessity for preserving the school's reputation and, therefore, their own opportunity for personal, family, and career success. It is something of an educational "Hawthorne effect." People everywhere, but especially in Japan, behave differently when they know that they are being watched and studied.

In retrospect, I am not surprised by the unruly behavior of young people at any level of education in Japan today, or anywhere for that matter, considering the strict authoritarian environment that they face throughout their early school years. Repression breeds frustration, resentment, and rebellion. And it serves as an unintended model for imitative behavior. Repression contributes nothing to reason nor to the skills or logic of persuasion.

Thus, when the authority structure is relaxed, weakened, or removed, young people find themselves inexperienced in personal decision making, lacking sensitivity to others, and in need of positive personal and social values. The result is turmoil—the kind of turmoil that drove Shikagawa to suicide.

9

BULLIED TO DEATH

I hate school. Everybody tries to cut you down. But I hate the teacher most
of all, because she gets you when you're down and then tramples all over
you.

—Junior High girl's suicide note

When a popular teenage singer, Yukiko Okada, leaped to her death
from the seventh floor of her agent's building in April 1986, it
seemed to point the way to an acceptable escape for many young
people who were suffering in a private world of senseless misery.
In less than three weeks after Okada took her life there was a rash
of suicides. One hundred and fourteen youth, including fifty-two
girls, killed themselves in April alone.

By the end of the year, the number of youths who jumped off
rooftops doubled. Others burned themselves to death with kero-
sene or jumped in front of bullet trains.

One sixteen-year-old girl told her sister just before leaping from
the thirteenth floor of her apartment, "I want to be like singer
Yukiko Okada."

Another depressed victim wrote, "It's not that I feel sorry for
Yukiko Okada. I just think it's the best method" (Kumiko
Makihara, "Suicidal Youths Following Idol Singer to Their
Deaths," *Asahi Evening News*, 4-23-86).

When All Else Fails . . .

For several years the suicide rate of young people under the age of nineteen had been declining in Japan, but suddenly jumped by 44 percent from 557 to 802 in 1986. Suicides by teenage girls rose an alarming 77 percent. These figures are most prominent in a rising wave of suicide throughout Japan, where the incidence in the population as a whole rose 8 percent to 25,524, the highest level in postwar history. (" '86 Suicides Highest in Postwar History," *Japan Times*, 4-17-87).

"Unlike American children," said Tamotsu Sengoku, director of the Japan Youth Research Institute, "Japanese kids hold in all their frustrations. They are under a lot of pressure from school and need to vent their energy in some way." He continued by saying that when everything else fails, suicide is the final outlet.

Some attribute these deaths to the intense pressure of examinations, which frequently begins as early as kindergarten. This is partly supported by statistics that show that suicides rise in March and April after examination scores are reported.

The pressures are great because the prospects for a student who fails the examination are grim, indeed. "We are a *gakureki shakai* [school society]," declared Hiroko Sato. "Your school is so important to your position in society. It is especially important to the most prestigious positions, those of government.

"At the Ministry of Finance, for example, twenty-three or twenty-five new executives are hired each year from Tokyo University. In fact, nearly every major corporation measures its size and importance by the ranking of the schools from which its new recruits will come every year.

"So the students are intent on passing the exams in junior high so that they can get into the best high school and have a better chance at the top college. Unfortunately, they can apply for only one college, and they are given only one chance a year to pass the grade," said Sato.

"In Hakodate right now there are one-hundred *chugaku ronin*, middle school graduates who don't have a high school." ['Ronin' was a term borrowed from earlier days: a samurai who roamed the countryside without a lord].

"The kids today, fifteen years of age, didn't get into the high ranked public or private school they hoped for. The best public and private schools in Hakodate are probably about the same ranking, depending on the fields of study. Chubukoko is public and LaSalle is Catholic.

"They will stay at home and study or they will go to a special cram school for *chugaku ronin* so that they can retake the exam next year. Some will eventually give in and go to lower level private schools. There are quite a few lower level schools that will take them, but it's the sign of a bleak future."

She paused, then reiterated with emphasis, "Imagine, a hundred fifteen-year-olds sitting out a year of regular school so that they can get another chance! A few will miss again [and] try again or maybe give up. How pitiful!"

Continued Sato, "At the university level, the family will spend ¥100,000 per month ($760) to support their *ronin* son in Tokyo or Sapporo so he can get a part-time job and hire a tutor, hoping to get into the college that he wants. For a daughter, maybe it is less important."

Marked the Wrong Box

Most students will take the private school examinations as a back-up in case they fail the national university examinations. About 5 percent will rely entirely on a single shot at the government test. Many of them have been encouraged, or discouraged, by the computer printouts of sample test results that are read to them by their *juku* teachers, explaining their relative chance for passing at certain levels on the examinations. While the test is fairly accurate, there are some things it cannot predict.

Students who fall ill on the day of the examination are just out of luck. Ichizo Oshima explained to me a different disaster that befell him. It was every student's nightmare, and it happened to Oshima.

"I was top of my class at the best high school in the city. I used to coach a group of my friends in their studies. All of them were sure that I would get the best score and that, hopefully, we'd all be able to go off to medical school together.

"But in my haste on the exam I misplaced a mark on the computer answer sheet . . . like answering question number 4 in the box for number 3. So all my answers on the whole test were wrong," lamented Oshima.

"It was disastrous. There was no makeup or explanation. I studied at the *yobiko* [a private cram school for college] for a year, but when I took the test, my father's business failed so he couldn't afford to send me to medical school that year. Ironically, that *yobiko* was the best, most interesting school I ever had.

"I joined the army because they promised to pay me for my medical schooling. But after I was in the army a year they informed me that I'd have to wait eight more years before I could study medicine. Eventually I left the army and went to Hakodate University before I was too old to be accepted anywhere. I'm working as a parking lot attendant, ten hours a day. I'll probably never have a very good job now." He added with sadness, "I put a mark in the wrong answer box."

Oshima confided further that he had frequently thought of killing himself. The desire grew whenever he pondered the life of his high school chums and what his life might have been. Then he cheered up, saying philosophically, "Worry is life and delight."

"Why?" I asked.

Oshima was a student for whom I felt a profound respect. This wise, self-assured, complicated student won the nickname "Professor Oshima" because he taught me so much about the twists and turns of philosophy and life.

"Why?"

"Because if I'm dead," replied Oshima, "then I have no worry. So worry is life because there's always hope. Hope is desperate." It's all written down in my pocket notebook.

There is a darker view of life held by many. According to psychiatrist Hiroshi Inamura, an author of several books on suicide, junior high school youths tend to have a romantic view of death. Many believe that "even if a person dies, he lives somewhere else . . . or is reborn as an animal or another human being."

Such ideas, says Dr. Inamura, have been on the rise, especially among girls who see the world of adults as "evil." Thus, they are inspired to die so that "they can go to heaven and live beautifully" ("Japanese Rash of Teen Suicides," *Japan Times*, 4-16-87).

Family Secrets

Another psychiatrist, Akira Hoshino, claims that the lack of sufficient support systems outside of the family account for the high suicide rate. "It would be good if youths had a place to turn to when they don't get along in their families, at school, or with their friends."

Young people are even less likely to turn to teachers than to parents when in need of help. A survey by the National Police Agency found that 40 percent of the victims of bullying had been able to consult their parents, but only 20 percent had been able to consult their teachers. "Which leaves 40 percent probably living alone with their problems," said the editors of *Japan Times*. "It is out of that group, we dare say, that most of the suicides come" ("Two Waves, One Undertow," *Japan Times*, 6-19-86).

What about professional counseling? Parents and youths alike are loathe to turn to psychological counseling because any record of such assistance is a hint that there are mental problems within the family. Such a stigma could become a black mark on a youth's marriageability and thus affect the future prospects of the entire family line for years to come.

Since Americans have a very different outlook on marriage and ancestry, it is difficult to appreciate the importance that the Japanese place on the purity of the family register. Among good families that are preparing for *omiai* (arranged marriages), family backgrounds are scrupulously investigated by private detectives who are hired to sniff out family secrets, those that are not recorded in the official city register.

One close friend of mine confided the secret of his heartbreak years before. "Because you're *gaijin*, and because I'm saying this in English, I can tell you things that I'd never tell my best friend in Japan.

"Once I was very much in love with a woman . . . and she felt the same about me. We wanted to get married, and her family investigated me thoroughly. They must have checked every source about everything . . . was there ever any mental illness, was there any Korean blood, was there any link to the *eta himin* [nonhuman outcast class, remnant of an ancient caste system]?

"When the girl's parents found out that I was color-blind, they prohibited an engagement. Any physical defect will be carried in the family line and will mark the children forever. They just refused her permission. She had to go along with their wishes.

"Before long, the family found her the proper match, and they were married. It didn't last long, however. After a few years, and two children, she started calling me every week at work. She wanted to see me, but I refused. Finally she stopped calling. I still think of her sometimes, but it's past."

Silent Suffering

In the midst of a nation that is renowned for its tight social fiber and strong group cohesion, a great many people feel desperately alone and unable to speak. This "silent suffering" is, ironically, nurtured in Japanese culture as a great, noble virtue.

The movies, *karaoke* (songs bar customers perform at a microphone to background music and videos provided by the establishment), and novels are endlessly dark, lonely, sad tales of frustration and despair. "Why do so many Japanese like those themes?" I asked. The response time and again was, "They are more interesting and more realistic."

In 1980, a singing group popular with young people, named "Ruts and Star," did a remake of a 1975 hit called "Runaway." They kept the song title, rewrote the words, and blackened their faces with shoe polish when they performed. According to a teacher at one of the Hakodate high schools, the song reflected the feelings of the young.

"Runaway"

Runaway, I love you very much.
I'll take you somewhere.
We're going to a world where
We'll be all alone.
I want to hold you runaway
You also have been lonely
And you have lost your love.
I've been lonely, too,
So now let's love each other.

The town is dry, and it's a lonely town.
Didn't like our town,
Was like grating our nails.

The man who recalled the lyrics said that the music is somewhat light and lively, like music of the 1950s. "It represents the exhilaration of freedom," he explained. "It would be nice to be able to run away from it all, but of course it's impossible so the tone isn't serious. 'I can't run by myself,' says the singer, 'but I could if you want to—I will go too.' It's a simple love song."

On another occasion, I asked my students at the teachers' college, "What is the best way to protect a student from a bad teacher?" I can vividly remember one soft-spoken girl who replied, "A student in that situation should silently think bad thoughts about the teacher all throughout the year."

Silence, of course, is no outlet at all. And where this is practiced on a grand scale, there are bound to be widespread neuroses.

One-Fifth Neurotic

Neurosis is precisely what was suspected and confirmed by a research team from Chiba University Medical School. Toshio Sato, an associate professor at the psychiatry and neurology department, asserts that one out of every five senior high school students was found to have the same degree of anxiety as clinical patients with anxiety neurosis.

A psychological test, called a Manifest Anxiety Survey (MAS), was administered to 515 students from sixteen high schools. The survey contained sixty-five sentences such as

When I work, I am under tension.

My sleep tends to be interrupted, and I cannot sleep well.

I sometimes think that there are many difficulties that I cannot overcome.

I sometimes fear that something unfortunate may happen.

A score of thirty points or more would indicate that the individual suffered anxiety neurosis, according to the researchers. Roughly 20 percent of the students overall scored that high, and, at one school in the Tohoku region, 40 percent scored in the higher range.

The students responded that they were studying because others were studying, because their parents or teachers were forcing them to study, or because they felt pressed to pass the college entrance examinations. Half the students replied that it was psychologically painful or unpleasant to go to school.

Shinsaku Noju, a teacher at Arakawa Number Four Junior High School in Tokyo, commented that students at high schools that send many graduates to prestigious colleges find it very difficult even to make friends among other students because they constantly perceive each other as rivals in a pitched battle for the few seats in those colleges ("1/5 of Senior High Students Neurotic," *Japan Times*, 3-19-86).

One girl at Chubu High School in Hakodate was said to have been so pressured to do well on the college entrance examinations that for months she stayed up late every night cramming. Her neck became so sore from straining over her books that she arranged a sort of noose over her desk upon which to rest her chin to take some of the tension off her neck. It has been assumed that exhaustion set in and her head slipped through the noose, whereupon she suffocated to death.

Some students are suddenly sent into, or constantly live with, great anxiety, fearing that some minor infraction of the school rules may destroy their whole future. One of these was sixteen-year-old Hiroyuki Yokoyama.

Yokoyama was so shocked by the punishment he received at school one day that he was unable to talk to anyone or even to leave a suicide note. After being suspended from school "for an indefinite period" because of driving a motorcycle without a license, he hanged himself from ropes inside a vinyl plastic hothouse at his home in Onohara. ("Teenager Kills Self over Suspension" *Japan Times*, 4-7-89).

In reflecting on the suicide death of singer Yukiko Okada, one high school student, Izumi Furukawa, said, "My friends, we all talked about it after that and said how we've felt like doing it too. . . . We just get fed up with things."

Indeed, there is plenty of trauma with which to get "fed up." One high school girl suffered numerous beatings from a teacher who was in charge of her track and field club. Before killing herself, she left a note simply saying, "I'm sick and tired of being hit, and I'm sick and tired of crying."

A junior high school girl who continually clashed with her teacher left this suicide note, "I hate school. Everybody tries to cut you down. But I hate the teacher most of all because she gets you when you're down and then tramples all over you."

And then fourteen-year-old Koji Sakai took a nylon rope and hanged himself from a bridge. He left a note on his desk at home saying, "Goodbye. Please ask my teacher about the details."

The "details" behind suicide usually involve a lengthy account of school bullying, of examination pressures, and of desperation at not being able to find help. This has been understood by no one better than Ko Mori, a teacher for more than twenty years at Tokyo Metropolitan Toshima High School and a private school, Seiko

Gakuin High School. Mori provides the most compelling explanation of the seeds of violence in the schools:

> Physical punishments administered these days entail humili-
> ation and are insidious and harsh. For example, a pupil who
> has forgotten something is made to lie supine on the floor with
> both legs raised, and the teacher sticks thumbtacks into the
> backs of his legs. Or a pupil who has not cleaned the class-
> room well is made to lick the bathroom floor.
>
> Such incredible punishments spark bullying. That is, the
> insidious nature of corporal punishment is reflected in pupils'
> behavior.
>
> The degeneration of teachers to such an extent can be
> attributed to the school system itself. Unlike at companies,
> there is almost no hierarchy at schools nor is there competi-
> tion for promotion. As well, a person fresh out of college is
> treated as a full-fledged teacher as soon as he joins the faculty,
> so he rarely suffers indignity or frustration.
>
> Under such circumstances, a teacher may not be able to
> share the pain of his pupils. Moreover, many teachers are not
> fit to be teachers in the first place. Many had good academic
> records during their college careers and thus are incapable of
> understanding the feelings of students who do poorly.
>
> Adding to the problem is the fact that even if a teacher does
> not properly deal with his [or her] pupils because of a defec-
> tive humanity or erroneous methods of teaching, no disciplin-
> ary action, such as a cut in pay or dismissal, is meted out to
> him. The fact that he is secure in his position probably makes
> him self-complacent and spoils him.
>
> A teacher influences students to the same extent as parents
> and siblings do. Lack of compassion, indifference and insid-
> iousness on the part of teachers who bear such heavy respon-
> sibility could be contributing to the problem.
>
> The schools, which emphasize study only, must be
> changed. Schools should by all means be institutions where
> children's potentials are nurtured. Regulations must be en-

forced to maintain order, and pupils must be made to understand this. But regulations now are enforced only to restrain pupils, and in many cases they work in an opposite fashion to disturb order at schools.

I would like to make a suggestion as a high school teacher: Improve the quality of teachers. From my experience, I know that there are many teachers who are not cut out to be such. There are many around me who are incapable of understanding pain and who have a perverted character.

The teachers' examination is a tough one. There are many who want to be teachers but cannot pass the examination, while persons of superior ability (scholastically, that is) do. However, having superior academic ability is not an absolute requirement for an educator. A teacher must share the life of his pupils and be able to understand their sufferings.

I strongly feel that teachers and the school authorities are to blame for bullying and not the pupils themselves (Ko Mori, "Rotten Teachers Create Rotten Kids," *Japan Times*, (12-22-85).

It is perfectly natural that young people will learn by imitating their elders, and if the young learn nothing else from brutal teachers, they learn how to bully their peers. The incidence of *ijime* (bullying) has been rapidly on the rise.

Late in 1984 the Ministry of Education scrambled to put together its first figures on bullying. Within a year parents were reporting three times as many cases, even though surveys demonstrated that parents were seldom told about the bullying by their children. This suggested that they had only examined the tip of the iceberg and that problems were reaching epidemic proportions.

10

SON OF *TAIBATSU*

Most kids we talk to say they feel refreshed after bullying another child. This shows the tremendous underlying pressure and frustration that they feel.

—Tamotsu Sengoku

From April to October 1985, a flood of 155,066 bullying reports came in across the nation. Thirty percent of these involved physical harm and the rest were deemed psychological in nature ("Survey Shows School Bullying on the Rise," *Asahi Evening News*, 2-22-86).

Of 5,825 police consultations early in 1986, up threefold from the previous year, 638 cases resulted in official investigations of assault, blackmail, and various forms of intimidation ("School Bullying Cases Triple," *Japan Times*, 4-14-86).

Of greater concern, the National Police Agency (NPA) found numerous cases of suicide and attempted murder. Violence and bodily injury accounted for 60 percent of the criminal cases. Extortion cases rose 65 percent over the previous year.

In 1985, minors aged fourteen to nineteen accounted for 43.4 percent of all criminal offenders, including adults. In the first eleven months of 1988, this figure increased to 48 percent.

According to a 1987 report of the NPA, nearly 54 percent of all murder cases and about 40 percent of robbery cases that were reported involved jobless minors ("Youth Crime up 100% over 1976," *Japan Times*, 8-23-87).

Going to the Streets

While education officials were patting themselves on the back for a decline in bullying in the schools during 1987 and 1988, statistics revealed that youth crime in general was still 100 percent greater than the previous decade. In addition, increasing truancy, absences due to sickness, and dropping out of school have been trends throughout the 1980s. It appears that frustrated young people have simply transferred much of their violence from the schoolgrounds to the streets.

Observed the editors of the *Japan Times*, "We have been aware of indications that a growing number of youngsters are opting out of the education rat race. Are we to exchange the problem of the 'examination hell' for increased juvenile crime?

"Actually, there has been a constant increase in crimes by jobless minors from 1980 to now. Also, there is a much higher proportion of heinous crimes—especially murders and arson—among this group" ("The Juvenile Crime Picture, *Japan Times*, 9-1-85).

The behavior of young thugs is not really very different from anything that one would expect from adult thugs or the mafia. The only real difference is the age and, perhaps, the level of sophistication.

Sometimes the youths are motivated by vengeance. One fourteen-year-old girl had been bullied or ignored by her classmates at Nomura Junior High, so she decided on revenge.

Assisted by another girl, she laced a batch of soup with paraquat, a deadly weed killer that can damage the lungs, liver, and kidney if ingested. Those eating the poisoned lunch discovered the plot but not before the teacher and eighteen of forty-two students in the class were injured enough to require hospital treatment ("School Lunch Soup Apparently Laced with Weed Killer," *Japan Times*, 5-28-87).

In another case, a fifteen-year-old girl was arrested in Sendai for the strangulation murder of her ailing mother. The girl's father had been sent by his company to live in another town. When she joined a group of unsavory companions, her mother scolded her for bad behavior.

With the help of one of these companions, the girl "punished" her mother for the scolding she had received. Then the two girls withdrew money from a bank and began planning to leave town. They were arrested at a game parlor and quickly confessed ("2 Teenage Girls Confess to Murder," *Daily Yomiuri*, 3-8-86).

Miniature Mafia

Sometimes the crimes are done for money. Fourteen-year-old Ken Kumazawa had been tormented by a group of students who had allegedly beaten him and extorted money from him on several occasions. At last, Kumazawa hanged himself inside a shed.

At Kita-Oshihara Junior High, a gang of six students had extorted up to $2,500 from about 120 of their classmates. According to investigators, the six boys called younger students into the hallway or lavatory during lunchtime in order to bully money out of them. These savvy young lads were simply putting into practice a lesson in raw majority rule they might have learned in a civics class.

And, just like the mafia, it can be quite tough on members of the gang who want out. Thirteen-year-old Chiharu Kameda jumped to her death from her family's condominium. Before jumping she arranged her room neatly and wrote, "I was threatened into bullying one of my friends. But I couldn't do it. Those two are the bad ones."

Gang members are sometimes punished merely for being insolent. Several members of a gang at Aoto Junior High in Tokyo accused young Ken Kurita of just that. He dared to tell the leader of his group that shoes should be taken off at the entrance to the house. The whole pack descended upon Kurita and began to kick and punch him. The boy finally died after they struck his head against a wall.

Some crimes are committed just for thrills. Forty-four students from Hikawa High School raided five souvenir shops near their skiing camps at Hakubamura. They were all arrested and ordered to stay home under "protective guidance" until authorities could figure out what to do with them. Classes at the school continued, even though there were only five students remaining in attendance.

This group from Hikawa High was more playful than most shoplifters of their generation. The police found that there had been a distinct change in the typical motives of young shoplifters over the last decade. Compared with youths in the 1970s, youngsters are stealing less for fun or on impulse. Now they have specific things that they want to get without paying. It is more premeditated, say the authorities.

Premeditation has also figured into the more serious, violent crimes as well. The Tokyo Metropolitan Police Department came to this conclusion following an investigation of the torture of a fifteen-year-old boy by two senior schoolmates. The bullies resented the fact that this boy was seeing a particular girl so they burned him with cigarettes in sixteen places all over his hands and back.

These two brutes were leaders of a group of ten others at school. In a search of their belongings the police uncovered a list of methods for torture: poking a hot needle under a victim's fingernail and forcing victims to eat insects. Other items of advice would have warmed the heart of any mobster or interrogator: "Don't leave evidence of the bullying," and "Don't kill a victim, but torment him slowly" ("Tokyo Police Report Cases of Bullying," *Japan Times*, 11-20-85).

Blood and Gore Department

As with young people in every industrialized nation, a lot of Japanese youth get their ideas from the movies and vice versa. One such movie to pick up on the contemporary scene was "Bii Bappu

Haisukuuru," ("Bebop High School"). Based on a best selling comic book this film, directed by Hiroyuki Nasu was best described in a review by Alan Booth:

> two Yokohama high school boys beat all their classmates silly while the soundtrack treats us to a song called 'Kick and Rush.' Then they smash each other to pulp, but recover in time to abuse their teacher, boot the shit out of an opposing rugby team, attack a rival gang with bats and chains and razors, smoke like chimneys, drink beer and shochu [similar to vodka] and whiskey, speak with little gobs of phlegm in their throats, and otherwise comport themselves in such a manner as to make one wonder whether Prime Minister Nakasone has not confused the necessity for educational reforms with an urgent need to extend the application of the death penalty. In one scene we see what is meant by 'bullying.' The culprits insert the pointed ends of a pair of chopsticks into their victim's nostrils and then smack the broad ends sharply with their hands, causing the membranes at the back of his nose to puncture and blood to spout out all over his face. This is certainly a vast improvement on forcing classmates to eat worms and other tame devices, and I expect the large numbers of high school pupils in whose company I watched the film will benefit from the hint. It is a good thing Japanese people keep reminding us what a peace-loving nation they are. Otherwise we wouldn't know what to think, would we? (Alan Booth, "Up Your Nose," *Asahi Evening News*, 1-7-86).

A film like this sounds quite repulsive to most adults. Perhaps one way to think of it is like a new sport. Surely these films give the same sense of release and relaxation that blood-and-guts boxing, wrestling, rugby, or football give to adult TV sports enthusiasts.

According to Tamotsu Sengoku, head of Japan's Youth Research Institute, "Most kids we talk to say they feel refreshed after bullying another child. This shows the tremendous underlying pressure and frustration that they feel" (Doug Stanglin, "Japan's Blackboard Jungle," *Newsweek*, 7-1-85).

More of this genre are the splatter videos that were as popular in Japan as in the United States. For teenagers who were trying to alleviate their boredom through gruesome fantasies, this was just the thing. "Junior and senior high school kids are by far our best customers in the blood-and-gore department," said a clerk at a video rental shop.

Most of the productions came from America, even those banned in the United States. Of one-hundred films released in 1985, only four were made in Japan. The first to be domestically produced, *The Guinea Pig*, was a forty-five minute portrayal of three men torturing a woman. At the climax, spikes were driven into her eyes.

Said the producer, attempting to avert criticism of his film, "Sex and nudity are out. We aren't porno video makers" ("Splatter Videos Are the Gory Rage for Teenagers," *Asahi Evening News*, 2-10-86).

Certain to attract a smaller audience, but of a more constructive nature, were films intended to sensitize youths to the trauma of *ijime*. One of these was *Yagate Haru*, or *Soon It Will Be Spring*.

One of the boys in the film was bullied by other students who finally realized his plight and tried to help him recover from injuries that were inflicted on him. Another victim is a girl who transferred from another school. She was ridiculed by a group of girls because of her poor apartment and because of her Yamagata dialect ("School Bullying Issue Generates New 'Ijime' Films," *Japan Times*, 3-24-86).

Dark Side of the Psyche

One thing the above film tried to expose was the difference in the way that boys and girls conducted their bullying. This was also the topic of a report by the School Bullying Special Advisory Group of the Tokyo Metropolitan Police Department (MPD). To no one's surprise, their examination of the issue found that the roles of bullies mirrored what the youth saw in magazines or on TV.

Boys are usually quite physical with their targets, punching and kicking them a lot. But they have also performed other tortures such as rubbing soap into the wounds of students, forcing students to smoke ten cigarettes at a time, or burning victims' skin with cigarette lighters. The list of imaginative techniques is limitless.

But it is the girls who really are the clever ones. They work their tricks on the psyche. They might kick their victims repeatedly, while singing a nursery song, or they might cut the hair of another girl so that she would look like a boy, according to the report.

Girls have had a particularly keen eye for the humiliating ritual. As described by Ko Mori, " 'Tea cloth wringing' is a typical insidious form of bullying perpetrated mostly at high schools. A girl's skirt is raised and the hem gathered together above the head so that the upper half of her body is completely covered by the skirt. When she is thus unable to freely move her arms, the bullies start attacking the exposed lower part of the body" (Ko Mori, "Rotten Teachers Create Rotten Kids," *Japan Times*, 12-22-85).

Most shocking of all, said the MPD, was the appalling behavior of adults. According to the bullies who were questioned, the teachers and parents pretended not to know what was happening . . . even when they saw the bullying occur before their eyes.

A prime example of this came to light in April 1989 when the remains of seventeen-year-old Junko Yoshida were found buried in a barrel of cement and left in an uninhabited area of Tokyo. Police traced down a boy who, with the aid of two friends, had lured the girl to a room in his parents' house.

There, the three boys kept the girl as a sexual prisoner for over a month, beating her and burning her hands and feet whenever she tried to escape. Finally, they killed Yoshida and disposed of her body.

Were the parents absent throughout this horror? No. The boy's father and mother witnessed the whole thing and even invited the girl to have dinner with them. The police reported that the parents "had once tried to talk the girl into escaping, but there is no evidence that the parents attempted to compel the boys to release her." News reports gave no indication that the parents lifted a finger to contact the police, nor that the parents were being charged with any crime ("Boys Accused in Death of Girl May Be Charged As Adults," *Japan Times*, 4-21-89).

Another, less brutal, case demonstrated how adults seemed to ignore the muffled pleas of children at moments of depression. When eleven-year-old Hiroshi Sugimoto jumped to his death from the top floor of a high-rise housing complex, no one claimed to know why he did it. In fact, such mystery surrounded his death that a special group from Yokohama National University was formed to determine the boy's motives.

The group reported that Hiroshi had been expressing a desire for death through his school compositions and paintings. For instance, one painting showed two faces in the shape of tennis rackets, one bright and playful the other dark and ghostlike.

The Yokohama fact-finding group claimed that the dark side of the painting was a futile expression of anger and frustration. According to them, these symptoms should have led the parents and the teacher to an early recognition of the boy's problems ("Adults Turn Blind Eye on School Bullying," *Japan Times*, 12-26-85).

The late Soho Tokutomi, journalist and critic, wrote an essay in 1939 saying that a person's situation may be unaccountable to friends, relatives, and teachers. Nevertheless, every suicide bears the minute evidence of "thousands of possible factors" that are involved. And, concluded Akira Tago, a psychology professor at Chiba University, what seems to be insignificant to an adult may be a tremendous burden to children who, according to Tago, do not understand the gravity of death.

Noh Mask Children

Still, the effort to read the signs of potential suicide may be futile. Some educational experts have warned that the spate of suicides in Japan is accompanied by an ominous rise in the number of "Noh mask-faced children," children hiding behind a seemingly wooden face mask. If one could judge by the news accounts of youth suicides, perhaps it is very difficult, but not impossible, to find warnings of a potential suicide ("Jottings," *Daily Yomiuri*, 3-18-86).

When Masashi Ko killed himself his parents were stunned. He was a good child; he read books, made friends laugh, was prankish, and talked often with his father. This was not the personality of one on the verge of death.

In retrospect, however, Masashi's parents believe that they discovered sure signs of their son's anguish. The boy's classroom compositions had changed significantly just prior to his death, and he was reading books much faster than before. Were these reliable clues?

After Katsunori Takayama hanged himself in his room, his parents found a note saying he was depressed over the high school entrance examinations that were being held that day. Just as shocked as the boy's parents, his homeroom teacher said that she could not think of anything serious enough to cause him to commit suicide.

Kimiko Sano hanged herself in a room with a vinyl cord around her neck. She had been stripped naked and beaten by five other girls. Acting upon complaints, the school held a meeting of her class, and all her classmates were reported to have "shown understanding." Even though the girl avoided going to school whenever possible, the principal said that he thought the problem had been settled.

Ten-year-old Kiyomi Mitsuhashi was a cheerful, polite girl who was popular at school and not a target of bullying. Yet she hanged herself from an iron bar in her study. Police think it may be related to embarrassment over an assignment that she forgot to hand in.

Masatoshi Saito hanged himself in his study, too. The study is such an appropriate mausoleum for these young people to choose. It is the study room that had become a prison, depriving them of access to real life beyond its walls.

School authorities noticed nothing extraordinary about Saito's behavior and said that he was never a target of bullying. It appears that the boy was despondent about his studies. He was doing so poorly in his grades that he thought he would never be able to have a career in auto manufacturing after his graduation.

Junko Uchida jumped from the eleventh floor of her apartment building when she became distressed over a two week bout with whooping cough and pneumonia.

A boy from Nagasaki quarreled with his mother and then went to his room saying, "I am just worthless." He then rigged an air rifle to the door so that his father would shoot him when entering the room.

Fumihiko Asakawa died from a fall from the seventh floor of his family's condominium. He left no note and school officials described him as a healthy, quiet, ordinary student who did not skip classes.

Teachers have reacted defensively to allegations that they should have been able to detect symptoms of student depression and prevent the suicides. They claimed that, compared with teachers in other nations, they are overburdened and overworked. Thus the task of responding to student needs has been very difficult.

How Unique Is Japan?

School crises are not unique to Japan. Certainly violence, bullying, and suicide are just as menacing, if not more so, in other countries. Any good lesson that is derived from an examination of the ills of Japan may also apply to educational systems in other nations.

In 1982, Japan ranked sixth internationally for suicides of youths between the ages of fifteen and twenty-four. The number of deaths per 100,000 of this segment of the population was 20.5 in Australia, 17.9 in Finland, 12.3 in the United States, and 10.6 in Japan.

Obviously those who committed suicide were unhappy, but what about the general student populace? In 1985, after conducting its survey of fifteen years, the Management and Coordination Agency (MCA) claimed that for once a majority of young people in Japan were "satisfied" with life. This is not a revelation that should cause immediate jubilation.

What about all those years the majority of youths was telling pollsters they were dissatisfied with life? Is not youth the time of life that should be somewhat carefree and happy? "When will it get better?" these youths might reasonably ask.

As *taibatsu, kanri kyoiku,* and *ijime* reached a crescendo on the nation's campuses, the percentage of young people who were dissatisfied with life dropped to a minority at 43 percent. What does that mean? Is the poll an accurate measure of satisfaction or dissatisfaction with life? And what difference does a poll make to the youngster who dies?

Are youths more satisfied when there is increasing regimentation and turmoil at school? Does the media distort the true picture and blow the troublespots all out of proportion? Were there political pressures to come up with one more survey that could offset the flood of unfavorable reports about the schools?

The statistics showed that Japan compared favorably with other countries with regard to youths' dissatisfaction with life. A similar international poll in 1983 showed levels of youth dissatisfaction at 55 percent in America, 54 percent in Britain, and 64 percent in France. How comparable are these figures? Is it possible to quantify and measure such things as satisfaction? Compared with what? The only true measure of satisfaction occurs when there exists an unhampered freedom of choice between alternatives. To the extent that choices are diminished for young people, vague measures of satisfaction become meaningless ("Majority of Youth Content with Life," *Daily Yomiuri* 1-16-86).

International comparisons are dubious at best and, at worst, serve to sidestep the real issues at stake. Comparisons are frequently used to excuse abusive attitudes toward young people if it can be shown that the conditions are worse in some "rival" nation. Clearly, all nations have a lot of improvements to make.

A further complication is that the surveys are usually comparing situations that are as different as apples and oranges. Japan has been characterized as having a much more homogeneous population than other nations. It tolerates a higher degree of corporal punishment than some nations, and there is an unusually strong incentive to keep matters secret, out of the courts, and, perhaps, out of the polls.

International comparisons are, nevertheless, tempting. A comparison of teachers' work responsibilities in the United States and Japan lent credence to the teachers' argument that they were too burdened to do much counseling. The Japan Youth Research Institute demonstrated that Japanese junior high instructors worked more overtime, covered a bigger curriculum in a shorter time, and were expected to supervise more students more thoroughly than their counterparts in the United States.

Teachers on the Verge

The incidence of bullying was reported to be slightly higher in America, but the breadth of teacher responsibility was greater in Japan. While bullying was said to occur in 84 percent of U.S. schools in 59 districts, bullying was noted in only 73 percent of Japanese schools in thirty-seven districts, and in 80 percent of schools in the major cities. Couple these statistics with the fact that Japanese classes averaged twice the size of American classes and one realizes an explosive situation.

In addition, 76 percent of the Japanese said that they frequently put in overtime work, whereas only 57 percent of the American teachers reported the same. Eighty percent of Japanese teachers declared that they were covering too much material, compared with only 13 percent in the United States.

Conversely, more U.S. students ranked their teachers highly, and 42 percent of the U.S. teachers said that they were often asked for advice by their students. Only 13 percent of the Japanese teachers said that they were frequently asked for advice ("Teachers Here Work Harder than in U.S.," *Japan Times*, 2-16-86).

In some cases, the pressure is so great that the teachers break. Tetsu Honda was a junior high school teacher in Saitama Prefecture who had forced a female student in his class to sit upright on the veranda of a classroom during his art class. She had been wearing black socks, a violation of a school rule.

The school principal heard of the punishment and, responding to a directive from the Ministry of Education that corporal punishment not be given in the schools, reprimanded Honda. Unable to cope with the scolding, Honda jumped to his death from the roof of the five-storied school ("Teacher Rebuked, Jumps to Death," *Japan Times*, 2-23-86).

Violent pressures on the teachers can come from the students themselves. One day at Yamate Junior High, for example, a homeroom teacher was lecturing his class saying, "If you don't lead a sober life, you will be isolated from others and become like that group." The group of eight third-year students that the teacher was referring to got wind of the teacher's lecture and, taking offense, charged into the faculty offices and demanded an apology.

When the teacher refused, they hit and kicked him, threw his papers on the floor, and fought with some ten other teachers in the room as well. Finally the teacher knelt (some reports say he prostrated himself so that his head touched the floor) and apologized. The teacher later explained that he agreed to apologize "in order to avoid any further confusion" ("8 Junior High Thugs Attack 10 Teachers," *Japan Times*, 3-2-86; "8 Angry Students Hurt 10 Teachers," *Daily Yomiuri*, 3-2-86).

To Love Nature and Human Beings

The teachers were not at all pleased with the situation in the schools, and their union leadership was quite outspoken in attacking the status quo. Ichiro Tanaka, Chairman of the Japan Teachers' Union, was unreserved in his criticism of the educational hierarchy. In the process, he did not deny that teachers had a role in the situation— although he stopped short of saying the teachers were responsible for creating the problems.

Tanaka told the Education Minister that the problem of school bullying stemmed from the heavy emphasis on entrance examination competition and that children were shackled by the controls of school authorities. He went on to say that teachers have a major responsibility for solving the problem ("Government, Nikkyoso to Tackle Bullying Issue," *Japan Times,* 2-28-86).

Two months later, in a speech to 200 teachers, parents, and educational experts from western Japan, Tanaka declared that the current "dehumanized education" was primarily responsible for the increasing volume of cases involving juvenile delinquency, dropouts, and suicides.

At the same meeting a junior high school teacher reported that 43 percent of his students had been bullied and that 45 percent admitted to bullying their classmates. If one assumed that the two groups did not overlap, not necessarily a valid assumption, then 88 percent of the students, or nearly everyone in the class, was in one group or the other. The parents of these children could not have been blind to a crisis of that magnitude ("Bullying Issue Mulled at Special Meet," *Japan Times*, 4-2-86).

Parents were not blind to the crisis; they were even more direct than Tanaka in placing the blame at the teachers' doorstep. A survey of 3,000 eligible voters around the country showed that nearly three out of four, or 73 percent, were dissatisfied with the current educational system; only 20 percent said they were satisfied—not at all what would have been expected by those of other nations who were so eager to import the Japanese educational system.

What was dissatisfying?

Bullying	56.7 percent
Teacher Quality	53.6 percent
School Violence and Delinquency	48.6 percent
Crammed Education	38.5 percent
Moral Education	36.0 percent

When asked about the reform proposals by the prime minister's special Education Council, the greatest number, 78.9 percent were pleased with a measure concerning moral education for discipline and teaching pupils in the primary schools to love nature and human beings ("School Education Gets Negative Vote," *Daily Yomiuri*, 3-11-86).

If "teaching pupils to love nature and human beings" could have been done through compulsion and force, the schools would have accomplished it long ago.

Bully Prototype

The chief of Hakodate's reformatory, Akio Sugasaki, spoke to a meeting of the Hakodate PTA one evening, recounting statistics about the number of young people in the reformatories and the violations for which they were being held. Interestingly, he seemed to have been trying to reassure the audience that bullying was a natural phenomenon.

Sugasaki declared bullying had always existed, especially among men who wanted to exert their power over the weak. Also, it existed as a way to socially ostracize others and was common in the Japanese army and navy where subordinates were often hazed by superiors. Bullying was also a frequent occurrence in prisons, especially toward newcomers.

In short, bullying was the equivalent of discrimination and prejudice, said Sugasaki. He then commented that there were four types of *ijime*: (1) child-to-child; (2) teacher-to-child; (3) child-to-teacher; and (4) teacher-to-teacher.

Sugasaki declared that child-to-child bullying was the greatest problem.

Listening to his lecture, the author was impressed that Sugasaki saw all of these interactions as the same thing: bullying was the equivalent to discrimination and prejudice and existed among all age groups. Quite sensible. But there was still room for disagreement with Sugasaki.

Discrimination and prejudice were certainly essential ingredients, but the activating elements—the ones that really mattered—were power, intimidation, and the use of or potential for force and violence. Without these elements, discrimination and prejudice were impotent.

Furthermore, the biggest problem was not the bullying of child-to-child. How could that be, if adults were the ones responsible for creating the world in which bullying took place? Adults must recognize their own varied forms of bullying and the impact that these have on the young. One would never find the solution to child-to-child bullying until one found the solution to bullying by the people whom children imitate. After all, imitation is the most fundamental method of all human learning.

Later in the meeting, Shooji Teraoka, an education specialist with the Hakodate Board of Education, gave a rather clinical description of the typical bully and his victim. "The father is weak and frequently absent," said Teraoka, "so his mother plays both the maternal and paternal roles when the child is young. A father's way and a mother's way of scolding are usually different, so a mother has to play both parts.

"The elementary school child appears to the teacher as the kind of child the mother wanted. But the mother can't very easily show a child the limit of fighting," stated Teraoka, "and this becomes a problem when the child makes it into junior high. As the child becomes stronger, he doesn't know where to stop his aggressive behavior, and the mother can neither know what to do nor can she show him how to stop.

"Also, there is a problem from mothers who push their kids to achieve too quickly instead of letting them do things by themselves. You mothers," he said to the audience, "shouldn't do things for them. Don't always push the kid too much to get good marks."

This advice was echoed by Shuji Honjo, who made a report to a convention of psychiatrists at Nagoya University. Declared Honjo, many of these bullies had been obedient to their parents as infants, especially to their mothers, but they thus became unable to make decisions on their own. Overprotective parents and too much emphasis on academic achievement seem to have resulted in much truancy ("Truant Children Who Become Violent and Sick on the Rise, Study Show," *Japan Times*, 5-24-86).

Teraoka also gave a clinical analysis of the characteristics of individuals who are the easy victims of bullying.

	Junior High	Elementary
1. Selfish	75 percent	52 percent
2. Too proud	72 percent	
3. Dirty	60 percent	54 percent
4. Timid	45 percent	44 percent
5. A loner	44 percent	
6. Weak or small	37 percent	43 percent
7. Slow	36 percent	51 percent
8. Not always great	33 percent	31 percent
9. Too serious	31 percent	26 percent
10. Top student	25 percent	27 percent
11. Bad at exercise	22 percent	37 percent
12. Not studious	14 percent	27 percent

Types of bullying fell into these categories, undoubtedly with considerable overlap:

1. Teasing	78 percent
2. Ignoring	57 percent
3. Tricking	52 percent
4. Violence	32 percent
5. Extortion	7 percent
6. Other	52 percent

"Some children don't know how to fight, so they can't resist," asserted Teraoka. "Many are seriously affected because friends bully them, and, afterward, they never want to have close friends again.

"And many of their friends seem to be immobilized, not able to help even if they wanted to. Usually, those surrounding the victim fall into these categories according to their involvement with the victim."

5. Not interested
4. Think it's funny
3. Helps the bully
2. Bullies
1. Victim himself

Finally, Teraoka told the parents that they could not rely on the children telling them directly of their problems at school. "As kids get older, they are generally less and less inclined to tell their parents about *ijime*." So watch for the symptoms of a child who has been bullied.

He is mad at everything.

He will do something for the first time.

He will refuse to go to school.

He will pretend sickness.

He will ask for money.

He will not go out often.

He will tell a lie.

This list of warning signs probably left all of the participants in the audience convinced that their children were in grave danger. Surely it would be difficult to find a child who has not done any of these things.

There was one overwhelming thought that went through my mind during the entire two-hour meeting. The speakers were both male, the master of ceremonies was male, most of the other twenty males present were teachers, but most all of the 160 silent audience were female.

Following the meeting I went to the home of a friend, a professor at one of the local universities. I mentioned some of the speeches that were given in the evening, and he gave me his version of what was at the root of this problem in the schools.

"In the old days," said Hashimoto, "many brothers, sisters, and cousins were around the house to help a youngster in trouble. All lived in the same community. Today, families are much smaller and they move more often.

"Before the war, typically there were ten children in a family. In fact, the government insisted that families have a lot of children. If they had more than ten, the government gave a celebration and certificates.

"Also, there were lots of helpers around the home—maids, servants, governesses," said Hashimoto. "And in difficult times there was also a clustering of everyone and their families into a sort of extended family.

"We always felt that big families were good, especially with medicine as bad as it was. Three of my brothers and sisters died in their first year and another died at age six."

As good as things appeared in the old days by comparison, it was not always easy to tell how close a family really was.

Fumie Kumagai, a sociology professor at Sophia University, analyzed filial violence in the Japanese home and agreed that such violence seemed to be on the rise throughout the 1970s. But the characteristics of that violence made it difficult for outsiders to identify.

For one thing, filial violence was not openly discussed until the 1970s, and this may not have been due to an increased incidence, but because of an increased willingness for a few families to come forward and to seek professional assistance.

"Who are the abusive children?" asked Kumagai rhetorically. "The abusive children are violent only within the family where privacy is strictly protected. Therefore, these abusive children are often regarded by such outsiders as school teachers, peers, neighbors, and even relatives as 'good children' who do no harm to society. They are quite different from the juvenile delinquents who threaten and assault others. Children who commit filial violence are often good students at school and considerate to others" (Fumie Kumagai, "Filial Violence: A Peculiar Parent-Child Relationship in the Japanese Family Today," *Journal of Comparative Family Studies*, 12, no. 3 (Summer 1981).

11

HOMOGENEOUS SOCIETY?

The arrogant attitude of adults naturally influences children. With all the bullying taking place and the exclusiveness of Japanese society, which rejects other human races, Japan's future seems extremely dark.
—Tsuneko Shiohara

One problem with many Japanese, as with every other nationality, is that there is often a squeamish feeling in their gut when it comes to accepting human beings of other races and nationalities. In a conversation with Chris Bale, Director of Oxfam's relief effort for Vietnamese boatpeople in Hong Kong, he told me that the Japanese were the least willing to accept refugees for resettlement.

"To get Australians to accept refugees, for instance, is like squeezing blood from a stone," said Bale. "And the Japanese are worse."

The Japanese would like to think that theirs is a homogeneous society and that heterogeneity is a major handicap of other nations. Former Prime Minister Yasuhiro Nakasone made a remark in 1986 that exemplified the Japanese attitude on this matter.

The average level of intelligence in America, said Nakasone, was impeded by the presence of "quite a few black people, Puerto Ricans, and Mexicans" (Aron Viner, *The Emerging Power of Japanese Money*, p. 106). His blatant prejudice was immediately jumped upon by critics who pointed out that Japan is also a culturally heterogeneous nation of Ainu, Koreans, Chinese, Westerners, and so forth, although many in Japan do not wish to acknowledge it. Even if there were not many other races and cultures in residence, a society so conditioned to conformity would have to create chasms and castes based on those differences they could find—from subtle twists in one's pronunciation to the occupations of one's ancesters. A case in point is the impoverished girl mentioned in the previous chapter who was portrayed as having been the target of bullying in the film, *Soon It Will Be Spring*. She was bullied because her dialect set her apart. That was a mildly distinguishing characteristic compared with the kinds of traits that had set other children apart and had resulted in their being treated as "outsiders."

When diplomatic relations thawed between Japan and China, the two nations began to re-examine the horrible consequences that befell people of both nations during decades of war. When Japan finally surrendered in 1945, thousands of Japanese nationals were trapped in China by events.

In 1972, the Japanese government sponsored programs to allow 1,043 war-displaced Chinese of Japanese parentage to visit Japan in order to locate their relatives. Of that number, small as it was, 261 settled in Japan with their Chinese spouses and children.

Commented Yukio Yoshimoto, a Japanese language teacher at Kasai Elementary School in Tokyo, "For the adult returnees, Japan is their homeland which they have greatly missed, but for their children, Japan is merely a foreign country. It seems that postwar ordeal has not yet ended but has just started for these children."

The children are taught the Japanese language as soon as they can learn it, and they are addressed by their new Japanese names. Nevertheless, it is still difficult to blend in without trouble.

Go Home! Where?

Despite the irrationality of it, bullies have tried to make these children assume responsibility for the outcome of World War II. "Why do they bully me?" said thirteen-year-old Qing Youjun. "China and Japan were at war and Japan was defeated. So people around me have been somehow blaming me for Japan's defeat"

(Emiko Oki, "Chinese Returnees' Kids Face Hard Facts of Living in Japan," *Japan Times*, 3-2-86).

Eighty percent of such children in Tokyo suffered the cruel verbal attacks of their classmates. And in Yamanishi Prefecture the percentage of this population experiencing such abuse was nearer 60 percent. Many of these families have chosen to cluster in a few districts because they want to be closer to each other for support and because the children were rejected by many other schools.

According to Tsuneko Shiohara, "Many of those children had their desks kicked, had chalk thrown at them, or were repeatedly told they were 'filthy and smelly.' 'It makes me feel sick just to hear you're Chinese,' they were told, or 'Go back to China.' I was outraged to learn this.

"When Japan's prime minister visited China for the first time since the war, I was unhappy with his comment on Japan's invasion of China as being a 'regrettable incident.' Unless we look back on our mistakes and apologize from our hearts, mistakes are likely to be repeated.

"The arrogant attitude of adults naturally influences children. With all the bullying taking place and the exclusiveness of Japanese society, which rejects other human races, Japan's future seems extremely dark" ("A Dark Future," *Asahi Evening News*, 4-5-86).

Indeed, it was everyone's loss, not just that of those who were being abused. Commented Yoshimoto, "It is obvious that the age-old Japanese mentality to despise people from other Asian countries and their lack of open-mindedness are causing a tragedy not only to the returnees' children but also to Japanese people themselves.

"For returnees' children, prejudice against their homeland China is something hard to bear. And Japanese people are missing wonderful opportunities to have a contact with a foreign culture.

"You Must Not Stand Out!"

Others who experience the battle of acceptance are the children of Japanese businessmen living abroad. Increasingly, the 220,000

Japanese businessmen overseas are trying to break the custom of *tanshinfunin* and take their families with them.

There are more than 50,000 Japanese children living abroad, 70 percent of whom are the children of Japanese businessmen. These children are subjected to culture shock twice: entry into the foreign culture and the return to Japanese culture. The latter may be the more difficult.

Not only do many of these returning children have to relearn the Japanese language or beef up on it, they also have to learn the basics of greetings and social interaction.

These students have found that many of the manners and attitudes, which helped them to succeed with teachers and friends in the foreign country, could ruin their prospects in the environment back home. For example, the assertiveness and individuality esteemed among their friends in the United States made them outcasts among their peers in Japan.

One businessman who was scheduled to return from his assignment in London counseled his son, "Stay quiet when you go to Japanese school. Don't act the way you did in England. You must not stand out" ("Culture Shocks Hard on Overseas Japan Kids," *Daily Yomiuri*, 1-22-86).

This same advice applies to parents who must adjust to Japanese business practices upon returning. "The tall nail will get hammered down," said professor Masatsugu Kimura in explaining the ways to get ahead in Japan, "so people will try to stay low, so [as] not to be conspicuous. Talented people must wait to be noticed by others and formally drawn out.

"At Kyoiku Daigaku, for instance," recalled Kimura, "we had an election for dean, and nobody ran for the post. Several faculty were recommended, and these men sat and waited until a majority recommended them. The starting point comes from others. If one advocated oneself, then he's sure to fail."

Kimura sat silently for a moment, then added, "There are some exceptions. The present dean, from the political science department, actually initiated his own candidacy."

This seemed to be an acceptable approach at Hakodate University, too. In an election of the university president, names of faculty were recommended from the floor, but those interested in the job had tactfully been lobbying for the post long before the official election.

Discrimination against Japanese students returning from abroad was identical to that directed at bicultural children, even when language deficiency was not a factor. An exchange of anonymous letters to the editor in *Japan Times* illustrated the similarity of troubles.

Mr. A wrote, "My Japanese wife and I, an American, were forced to formally withdraw our son from a Japanese public elementary school. . . . Our son, whose first language is Japanese, had attended this elementary school for four and a half years. During this time he suffered physical abuse and much more painful ostracism. Incidents of teasing by students and even some teachers were exceedingly distressful. . . . Upon learning of this news (of the boy's departure) groups of our son's classmates got together and excitedly and joyously exclaimed, "We did it! We did it!" (We got rid of him) . . . I wonder if other families, similar to ours, have had a similar experience" ("A Difficult School Decision," *Japan Times* 4-5-89).

One reader responded, "In reference to the letter 'A Difficult School Decision,' let me put the parents' minds at ease insofar that their son was not ostracized because of mixed racial background, even though I realize that this does not change the situation.

"The Japanese school system insists on strict conformity, the same style short haircut, same school uniform, even how many centimeters a girl's skirt must be below the knee, etc. This is so impressed on the children from a tender age that they learn not to accept anybody who does not conform physically or mentally. In your case, physically, but it applies similarly to Japanese children returning from overseas who have learned different behaviors and whose Japanese may not be up to par, etc.

"There are many examples where teachers and principals do not tolerate such nonconformity, unfair as it may be. The same applies in the large Japanese corporations. Have you ever seen a young 'salaryman' with a mustache or, God forbid, a beard?"

Then this unnamed advisor added, unhelpfully, "These are the facts, and, if you live here, you have no choice but to accept them" ("Non-Conformity Isn't Tolerated," *Japan Times*, 4-12-89).

Odd Man Out

Are the children at these schools wrong to be critical of new-comers? Are they insensitive by making fun of foreigners or people with strange accents? Again, as in so many other situations, young people are simply imitating their elders.

Teachers treat other teachers with disdain if they come from faraway districts, behave awkwardly, or come from a university different from that of the majority of teachers. I was told that teachers sometimes start out at different pay levels or with favorable or unfavorable assignments, depending on the university from which they graduated.

Hiroko Sato observed, "The alumni of Kyoiku Daigaku are very powerful in Hakodate. One can't be a principal or vice principal without being a graduate of the college. These positions can also translate into political power. The vice mayor was once a principal of one of the schools."

Connections to an influential university network not only served to make political power, but also proved useful in breaking the power of those outside the group. "Even former Prime Minister Kakuei Tanaka was a victim of the old school system," observed one of my colleagues.

"Tanaka was more efficient at the game of political bribery than all the others, that's how he built and maintained his political machine. That was nothing new. The other party faction leaders did the same kind of thing all the time.

"What really irritated the others was the fact that Tanaka was the only prime minister not to come from Tokyo University. His rivals couldn't stand that. He wasn't one of them. So they let him fall. If anyone else had been implicated in the Lockheed scandal, which was really minor compared to the other domestic corruption of the day, then they would have found a way to cover it up."

Citizens Only

Another matter of discrimination that has long been festering, is the standing regulation that only Japanese citizens can be allowed to teach in the public schools. This phobia over noncitizens has not only led to interminable racial strife in Japan, virtually ignored by Nakasone, but also it has purportedly been the cause of some terrible incompetencies in the classroom, particularly in language training.

Many private schools have been able to attract students to superb English-language programs because they are able to hire native English speakers. Public schools have only been permitted to do this, within narrow parameters, over the past couple of years. Even with this new permission to open up the hiring process, public schools have been woefully slow at accepting foreigners.

The problem is all the more serious because Koreans, who may have been born and raised in Japan and whose parents were brought to Japan as forced labor during the war, can never qualify as Japanese citizens. Thus, these 700,000 Koreans are hounded every few years to keep up their alien registration cards and to submit to the rather humiliating exercise of being fingerprinted like criminals.

Since Koreans are not bona fide citizens, they cannot be hired as public school teachers. A couple years ago, the Ministry of Education interrogated a local education board in Osaka over the case of a twenty-nine-year-old Korean woman who had been hired as a Japanese language instructor.

This woman graduated from college in 1982 and worked as a part-time instructor until she passed the teacher's qualifying examination. Soon thereafter the local school board hired her as a full-time teacher, despite the government policy. A senior official of the local education board said that they did not want to defy the national policy, but, at the same time, they had to recognize that

Osaka Prefecture had the greatest number of Korean residents in the nation ("Hiring of Korean Teacher Against Ministry Directive," *Japan Times*, 5-18-87).

With official discrimination such as this, it is difficult to expect children to behave any differently toward outsiders. True, the children may not have read the newspaper accounts of official actions to learn about these ideas, but surely they hear bigotry expressed in the comments of their elders and they recognize the absence of different nationalities in their schools.

Young people rarely saw their teachers dealing with other Asians as equals on a daily basis. Instead, they grew accustomed to seeing foreigners as featured novelties on TV, along with documentaries on koala bears and freaks from around the world.

A list of various types of bullying that was compiled by the police uses terminology that gives the impression that bullying is something that only children do: playing tricks on the telephone, persistently making fun of other's shortcomings or defects, robbing property or money, shunning the weak, picking on the weak, beating and kicking the weak, and so on. Yet bullying by adults covers all the same territory and it is no less serious simply because the perpetrators are adult. Which is worse, (1) to shun someone at school for a year or (2) to cut an entire segment of the population out of work, marriage opportunities, and social standing for generations as has been done to the Koreans?

Untouchables

One class of society that the Japanese seldom care to talk about is the *eta himin* (nonhumans) referred to in an earlier chapter. They were the "untouchable caste" of old Japan who worked in slaughterhouses where normal people could not work. Consequently, it was their tradition to fashion leather goods and to eat meat, not done by ordinary Japanese.

At the top of society was the royalty, followed by samurai, farmers, craftsmen, and merchants. The *eta himin* were not even on the list and were compelled to live outside the city or in certain circumscribed areas.

"In the old days," said an acquaintance, "criminals or runaways would be safe if they could beat their pursuers to the *eta himin* districts, sometimes referred to as 'samurai villages' because so many Lordless samurai found their way there as well. It was a good place to hide, but one could never return [to accepted society].

"Even today," she told me, "ordinary folk never travel through these poor villages. They are not dangerous, it is just that they have such an association with the low life . . . and perhaps some unmentionable ancestral crime."

Information about a family from one of these villages is nearly impossible to hide today. The government insists on registration for everything: whenever moving from one city to another; when getting a driver's license, marriage license, divorce, passport, or a new job. The mere location of one's residence is enough to mark a family, affecting its whole future.

"One's family history could be found on the [registry] card, available to anyone who looked at it," she said. "Defenders of this policy claim that it helps make for a 'stable' society to know who has had a criminal record."

Private detectives sometimes make up a list of the descendants from this *eta himin* caste and sell it to people who are researching backgrounds for *omiai* (arranged marriage) or to companies that use it as a way of blacklisting employees. A diet member of the Japan Socialist Party (JSP) once accused a government subsidized bank of purchasing one of these lists from a bookseller. The bank tried to explain that they bought it as *giri* (a polite obligatory gesture) to their client but had no intention of using it when they placed it in their library.

Officially Respectable

During the Meiji era, the *eta himin* caste was made "officially" respectable. They were no longer to be called "*eta himin*" but instead were officially referred to as "new human beings," a revealing and distinct title in itself. And as a gesture of official support, their villages were razed and replaced by respectable public housing projects.

"Yet there is still widespread discrimination," said my woman friend about the *eta himin* who now number from one to three million. "Even in the schools there are obstacles for them. Technically the schools are free, but the PTA fee, the school support fee; and numerous expenses for books, bags, and uniforms put the cost out of the range of these people . . . so they don't go on."

The bank that was accused of discrimination by the JSP was finally compelled to demonstrate that it was in accord with the current national policy against discrimination based on social class or sex. So the bank authorities apologized for having the blacklist book and promised to make bank clerks study how wrong it is to discriminate.

"So every year now we must sit through a two-hour meeting to be tutored from headquarters on the evils of discrimination," explained an irate female employee of the bank. "It's all a facade.

"In the same meeting the top recruiting officer said that there is no discrimination in the bank on the basis of either sex or status. I would have objected to what he said in the meeting," she continued, "but the branch manager was there and he would have gotten revenge later.

"Even though they boast of lifetime employment with the bank, they have many ways of getting rid of employees without firing them. Sometimes an employee is sent to work as a clerk for a small client that is in debt to the bank, and eventually they are transferred to the other company's payroll. The client has to take the employee because of the influence the bank has over them.

"One friend of mine was thought to be associated with an effort to unionize the employees, so they exiled him to a small branch bank in the countryside. Others, called '*madogiwa-zoku*' [window workers], are just put next to the window with nothing to do. Or they might force a resignation through humiliation.

"For example, the manager might let his minions at the bank know that someone isn't wanted any more. The others might then speak down to that person until they leave. There are many ways to address someone with lower status words, which are really shameful. The individual gets the message quickly, and they are gone."

The woman went on to explain how she had been at the bank for twenty-seven years and at her age she felt locked into the job. No one would hire a woman of her age anywhere else, so she had to be somewhat careful.

She had just trained a new young male employee who had been at the bank less than a year. He was immediately given more responsibility than her, assigned to a bigger desk, and placed closer to the customers to lend an appearance of importance. But he still had to turn to her to answer every question. "Younger women don't feel the discrimination so much," she said, "but older women feel it because they should be senior to all the new young men."

Words Differ from Practice

Male recruits became managers within a couple years, even if they did not want to become managers. They did not all like the idea of becoming managers because those on the managerial track were required to move around the country. Some of those tapped for management preferred, futilely, to stay in the city where they grew up and where their extended families lived.

This woman, on the other hand, had the same education as many of the men and had always wanted to become a manager but was routinely denied permission to take the requisite training courses. Like hearing a broken record, she was told that it was better for her to stay in clerical positions so that she could remain in town and take care of her mother.

"When I joined the bank at the age of eighteen they required me to sign a document saying that, as long as I was single, I would always live with my mother and never live alone. The bank managers thought it would be bad for the bank's reputation to have female employees living alone. Now they use that same document to 'prove' that I'm not eligible for management because I promised to stay with my mother!

"Even if I could persuade my seventy-year-old mother to leave everything and go with me so that I could get a promotion, I couldn't expect an increase in pay. Men expect to be paid more because they are responsible for a whole family. So they say, 'Why should a woman get it?'

"The bank manager used to tell me that the law forbade women from working past eight o'clock in the evening," she said. "He explained that the law was for the 'protection' of women and of the family. And since managers frequently had to stay at work much longer, the law made my promotion impossible.

"The new equality law won't change a thing. The equality argument is only used when it's convenient. Japan has a good constitution and laws, but they are often ignored because few people will challenge bad practices in the courts. And when a lawsuit is won by women in a bank, a small branch of the bank is set up comprised only of women."

Now that she was getting older, and at the top of the seniority scale, the bank officials were thinking of letting her go because she was costing them too much for the low level of clerical work that she was assigned. She trembled as she said, "It's not my fault that I haven't been given more responsibility. But they'll use that to get rid of me now."

With a touch of bitterness in her voice she said, "This is all so foolish because the man who was lecturing us about discrimination discriminates himself! He is blind to how women feel, but he is used to the Japanese way...words and practice are different."

Saying one thing and doing another is not unique to the Japanese. What is somewhat unique, however, is the degree that Japanese use pressures like these to enforce tight group conformity. This group cohesion is cited as one of the key elements in the success of the Japanese educational and managerial systems in recent years.

Those Americans who are most impressed with this kind of group discipline in Japanese schools and workplaces will speak mysteriously and admiringly about the deep roots of this behavior in the country's historic and cultural past. The origins of "group-ism," however, are neither mysterious nor entirely admirable.

12

SHOGUN'S GHOST

Everyone has a different character and different home conditions. Hence, it is impossible to force changes through joint responsibility. It was unbearable for me to be punished for something I was not responsible for.
—Reiko Takahashi

I have heard people in the United States say that the Japanese are naturally group-oriented people, whereas Westerners are naturally individualistic. My Japanese friends tell me that this is too simplistic.

"We Japanese have long enjoyed sumo, judo, kendo, go, and shogi, which are all one-on-one games. It was only following the coming of MacArthur that we adopted western team sports like baseball, volleyball, and basketball," said one friend of mine. Then he added with a chuckle, "You Americans are too group oriented!"

The chuckle was acknowledgment, nonetheless, that the usual perception of the Japanese is that they are very group-oriented compared with most Westerners. But group behavior does not indicate a lack of individual thought or ability. It merely means individual expression is suppressed and kept secret, a very carefully guarded secret.

"In English, the word 'I' is always capitalized and used constantly," explained Yamazaki, my Japanese language tutor. "Chinese and Japanese don't have capitalization, but the Chinese will still use the word for 'I.' But in Japan we will skip it. We want to be thought of as part of a group. Americans think the 'I' is very important. The Japanese skip the subject."

The Japanese "I" is understood. It is hidden or skipped in conversation but not gone and not "inscrutable." There were very solid reasons for the Japanese to cultivate secrecy. This secrecy is the result of centuries of a particularly thorough form of state control. Living under the same control over a long enough period of time, Americans would behave the same.

All For One . . .

A phenomenon that is commonplace in Japanese schools is the practice of "joint responsibility." Thus, a whole group of people can be held responsible for the behavior of one individual member of that group. Likewise, one individual can be punished simply for associating with other people who are considered "bad." And a school's reputation can be tarnished, thus damaging all employees and students in the eyes of the whole community, if one of the school members does something dishonorable.

A high school teacher explained a recent situation that illustrated the point. "Eight junior high school boys were playing around with a bicycle one day when they were stopped by a policewoman. The kids said that they just found it and were just having some fun. Not believing them, the policewoman hauled them off to the police station.

"There had been a report that the bicycle was stolen, and the police found some tobacco on the boys, so they were in trouble. Usually the first thing the police do is to notify the school, even before calling the parents. It holds true for the high school kids, too. That's why I take turns with all the other teachers and stand duty in the school office, even on Sundays.

"While it was never proven that any of the boys actually stole the bike, it was still really shameful because their names appeared in the newspaper. Later," said the teacher, "when the students were about to graduate from junior high, they applied for admission into some of the local high schools but were turned down. After hunting around, three of the students finally went to some lower level public schools, but the other five had to leave town before they could find a school in the countryside that would take them.

"Country schools don't have quite as good a reputation, so the future will be be more difficult for those kids. That simple incident over the bicycle ruined their lives . . . and, to a great extent, that of their families as well.

"Almost anyone can enter some of the private schools in town, unless the student has reputation problems. Even students with very high grades in junior high won't be allowed to take the admissions tests if they appear to be a risk to a school's image.

"As a result of this kind of treatment in the schools, a lot of people, even some at Family Court, are now afraid to tell the school officials when a kid gets into trouble. They are afraid that the school would just suspend the student and ruin his life. So what help is that to the kid?"

I asked him, "How serious is a damaged reputation to a school?"

"Let me give you an example. Yuto High School is very nervous about its reputation because of what happened in 1982, just a few weeks before graduation," he replied. "One student on the school baseball team was the driver in a hit-and-run accident in which a girl was injured. As a result the whole school had to take responsibility.

"That year their baseball team was number one in Hokkaido and was ready to go on for the national championship. That meant a lot to everybody at the school.

"But, because of the car accident, they had to forfeit the tournament. It's also the tradition of the baseball association: If any member of a team does anything against the rules, then the team can't play. This covers all teams in Japan. The association can force a school to forfeit.

"The baseball association is very powerful, and they argue that baseball is rather unique. The logic behind this kind of ruling is that baseball is not an individual sport. If any one member has an accident then the whole team must take responsibility.

"So the school tries to prevent such things from happening by carefully screening out anyone with a bad mark on their record."

The Tall Nail Gets Hammered Down

In Japanese schools, it is typical for the students to stay in one room and for the teachers to move from class to class. One teacher, a foreign English language teacher at a girls' junior high school, came into the classroom and asked the girls how they did on the history test they had taken in the previous class period. She told me that she was shocked by their answer.

"Every girl got a zero!" recalled the teacher. "I asked how they could all have gotten zeros. The girls told me that because one of the students had cheated, they all had to take zero scores. What really disturbed me was that they didn't seem to be the slightest bit upset that they all had to take punishment for one student's cheating.

"Later that month, with about three weeks left before the final exams," said the woman shaking her head, "the same history teacher decided to punish the whole class because one of the students forgot to bring her textbook from home that morning. So the history teacher gathered up all the textbooks and piled them in the schoolyard outside.

"Then she burned the whole stack of books," the teacher reported with a gasp. "The punishment? The students were going to have to study for the exams without their books!"

The intention of the teacher was to enlist the assistance of all the other punished students in the task of enforcing the rules. Since everyone can be made to suffer for the actions of a few, it is everyone's immediate concern that nonconformity be quashed.

The pervasiveness of this attitude goes a long way in explaining why young toughs "lean on" those who are different, why innocent bystanders rarely come to the defense of misfits, and why, in Ko Mori's words, "Teachers do nothing about bullying but try desperately to prevent it from becoming known outside the school.

Student bullying is frequently the action of young jackals who reinforce the hostility that some teachers have toward students who are different. New students, students with long hair, or even students who challenge the teachers' authority are all easy marks for these teacher groupies.

At a junior high school in Fujioka City, three students were kicked and punched by five others after two of the victims called for free speech in the student council. The bullies accused the others of "being cheeky" for daring to suggest that the student council should be a place where anyone can express his or her opinions freely.

Two of the victims were running for election to the student council, and the other was president of the tennis club. They tried to hide their injuries in order to avoid reprisals. But the beatings were severe and resulted in five days to a week of treatment.

"Silence Is Proof of Suppression"

Reiko Takahashi, an elderly housewife from Akita City, explained how this kind of punishment is at the root of the problems of violence in the schools. "Everyone knows that bullying by teachers is conducted almost every day at schools in the name of 'guidance.' It seems that the bad practice of the prewar years has not disappeared in forty years.

"I recall my humiliation during the war, when I was still in elementary school," said Takahashi, "Under the principle of joint responsibility, a group member's mistake was the group leader's responsibility, and class misdeeds were the responsibility of the class leader. Naturally, everybody received a shower of punches for whatever reason, whether girl or boy.

"Everyone has a different character and different home conditions. Hence, it is impossible to force changes through joint responsibility. It was unbearable for me to be punished for something I was not responsible for."

Observed Takahashi, "Children nowadays may perhaps try to get their vengeance by bullying the child who actually caused the misconduct. Irrational rules and corporal punishment only cause repulsion.

"Formal obedience accumulates dissatisfaction. The children's silence is proof of their suppression to disagree" (Reiko Takahashi, "Restrict Corporal Punishment," *Asahi Evening News*, 11-30-85).

Five-Family System

The roots of this enforced "groupism" are not mysterious. A specific system of control was introduced into Japan by rulers who intended to regulate nearly every aspect of life. So thorough was the repression, that every form of modern totalitarian rule pales beside it. And it lasted for so many hundreds of years that its effects became permanently lodged in the fabric of Japanese culture.

It is called *goningumi*, (five-man system). It is a system that calls for each member of a group to be held responsible for the actions of all others in the group.

Goiningumi is thought to have originated in China during the Tang Dynasty, toward the end of the Muromachi Period (1400–1554) in Japan. With the introduction of firearms into Japan, fighting styles changed and the structure of the army changed along with them. For the first time, troops were assigned to groups of five to ten soldiers each.

Hideyoshi Toyotomi (1536–1598) adopted the system for the servants and guards at his residence in the central region of Japan. When civil war broke out, the system was used as a form of security by applying it to families in the general populace.

At the beginning of the Edo period (1603–1867), *goningumi* was first used by the central government in order to prevent unofficial robbery and to secure its own official robbery. Usually five families, but sometimes anywhere from two to ten families, were assigned to a group and each was responsible for all of the other families.

By 1637, *goningumi* was expanded into a full system of detailed rules which governed nearly every aspect of daily life; it was complete and widespread, existing in all the districts as the smallest organizational unit of the population. Its purpose was to secure the government, both internally and externally, and to fortify the feudal hierarchy ("Goningumi," *Nihon Rekishi Daijiten* 4, [Kawadeshoboshinsha Publisher, 1985]).

Commented Kazu Tomisawa, "The central government introduced a rigid class system which dictated behavior with regard to clothes, hair, manners, speech . . . everything. Members of a peasant family might be prohibited from wearing silk, a sash, certain shoes, trailing sleeves, bright colors, or even clothes with the wrong sized polka dots."

Everybody knew about everybody else and their status by means of the clothing they wore. A girl could be put into jail for several years for wearing bright colors that were not approved for her station in life. Conformity in appearance was thus a necessity.

"If someone didn't pay the rice tax or if a household took in a stranger, all members of the five families had to take responsibility," said Tomisawa. "In severe cases they could all be put to death. Strangers were seen as a very serious threat."

"A local daimyo, or feudal lord, ruled at the will of the shogun, head of the central government. If the daimyo was found to be doing anything against the shogun, then all his relatives might be required to join him in suicide and his friends would be exiled in order to make room for the new daimyo."

She explained that the shogun was always looking for a pretext to oust an old daimyo so that he could replace him with his own relatives. Therefore, the shogun started a spy network, the infamous *ninja*, to infiltrate the local fiefdoms and gather incriminating information.

Wary of this, and for good reason, the daimyo became very secretive and instituted rigid barriers against travel and severe punishments for harboring strangers or "criminals," such as Christians. If anyone gave assistance to outsiders, all five families could be killed.

Being Different Was to Be Dead

According to Yoshiaki Shoda, a faculty member of Gakushuin
High School in Tokyo, the *goningumi* really included a great
number of people; the five families were the extended family
groups. Considering only the male heads, their relationships to a
guilty party being punished might have looked like this:

1. father and brothers
2. grandparents and/or grandsons
3. granduncles
4. uncles
5. cousins

Of course the women and their children could be punished, too.
Said Shoda, "There were typically six to eight children in each
family in those days. So the number affected by some offense could
reach into the hundreds."

Even contemplating minor crimes, anything that deviated from
the norm, necessitated thinking of the entire family first. No one
made any trips; it was better to stay home than to take such great
risks. No one talked to strangers, and everyone kept their personal
lives, their individuality, well hidden.

Shoda explained that if one person in the group killed someone
or caused an injury that was nearly fatal, then the group could all
be put to death. Death for theft was based on the amount that was
stolen. It might be the equivalent of a million yen ($7,700) today.

"A samurai was governed by different rules," said Shoda. "If he
killed someone of lower status, well, then the determination of
punishment, if any, depended on the reason for killing.

"If his wife was found with another man, then it was considered
a cleansing of his honor to place one lover on top of the other and
kill them both with one stroke of the sword. A samurai's honor was
very vulnerable to actions by his family.

"For example, if a samurai's child stole even as much as one pencil," declared Shoda, "then he might kill both the child and himself because of the shame. So control of children had to be very severe at a very early age."

Commenting on the manner of control, Yamazaki said, "Japan is the 'Embarrassed Culture.' During the Edo period not all samurai could earn enough money to buy food. But such a person could not admit it. The embarrassment of one family member was the same embarrassment for all the family.

"In *hazukashi no bunka* [the Embarrassed Culture]," she went on, "there was no individuality, always group shame. And virtue for the individual was long suffering and patience. Even today a mother usually tells her children, 'Don't do that, it's embarrassing.' People find their tranquility in the tea ceremony. Then one can sit quietly and concentrate inwardly."

The manner of dealing with deviant children was further examined by Masatsugu Kimura, of the teachers' college in Hakodate. "A method of disinheriting family members originated in the Edo Era because of the closeness that was required by the five-family system," said Kimura.

"No single child must deviate. If one child was very bad, then he could get everyone into trouble. So the head of the family would declare the boy disinherited, an outcast.

"The family would even make him wear a special type of clothing and cap so that everyone could see at a glance that he was disinherited . . . or 'made into a stranger.' This way the family protected itself from accusations from the central government.

"Whenever there was organized revolt against the central government, for example, because of high rice taxes, the farmers still behaved as a group because their fate was all sealed together. They signed bloodpacts in which their names were arranged in a circle so as to conceal the leader.

"But these farmer rebellions most often failed and death was the common penalty. There were many cruel ways of torture at the time," sighed Kimura.

Romance Suppressed

"There were occasional violations of the rules because people still have energy," remarked Tomisawa, "but 300 years is very long." The Edo Period spanned 300 years and, through the steel grip of *goningumi*, solidified the social structure and rooted out rebellious tendencies.

Everyone was closely watched by everyone else—spying eyes were those of everyone familiar and unfamiliar, at home and in other villages. Everyone served as an adjunct to the police and turned each other over to the authorities for any deviations. Everyone made sure that everybody else paid their taxes and also paid full respect to the daimyo [lord].

The all-pervasive motive was fear. George Orwell could not have had a better model of absolute totalitarian manipulation when he wrote his classic novel, *1984*.

Outsiders were always suspect, and few ever dared to become an outsider by traveling unnecessarily. In fact, the surest safety was in cutting off the outside world entirely.

When Commodore Matthew Perry's ships first came to Hakodate harbor, the entire city was ordered to close windows and doors without daring to peek. The children were ordered evacuated from town. Japanese sailors who had been lost at sea, thus involuntarily coming into contact with foreigners, returned in great fear. They feared being put to death by the Japanese authorities because of contamination from the outside.

Any hint of being different was a threat to everyone's life and to the lives of all members of one's family. The pressure to conform was tremendous. No one even wanted the words to be spoken: "You are different!"

"This attitude even permeated married life," declared Tomisawa. "Individual taste was not part of the formula for marriage. Romantic inclinations had to take second place to family considerations.

"Romantic love still is not talked about by the older generations. Emotionalism disturbs many rules so it is a sort of sin. Kabuki theater had many love stories, but it was separate from real life.

The arts frequently expressed what the common folk were afraid to reveal about the hidden side of their own lives. For instance, the people of Hakodate have long paid homage to the poet Takuboku Ishigawa (1886–1912) who resided a short time in their town. His statue now graces one of the most scenic parks along the beachfront, and formal dinners are given to honor his memory. One of Takuboku's quotations was recently engraved on a massive five-foot granite stone beside the house where he lived, "Those who are frustrated in their endeavors, come drink sake at my house."

Yet everything in Takuboku's own life represented a life style that would have been considered shameful if the townsfolk had lived that way themselves. He was punished as a troublemaker in high school for cheating on examinations, for loving a girl, and for numerous other offenses. He finally dropped out of school and never earned a diploma.

Takuboku never could find a very steady job. One year, he changed jobs six times, moved all over the country, and lived off his family and friends. Later, he married his childhood sweetheart, then deserted her and carried on numerous affairs. He was an alcoholic, was always impoverished, and dallied with radicals. Eventually he died at a young age from tuberculosis.

So why was Takuboku so revered by the respectable upper crust of Hakodate who appeared at the dinners and contributed generously to the memorials? How could they speak so reverently of a man whose behavior would have brought shame if they, or members of their families, had behaved in the same manner?

"Takuboku moved many people," answered a colleague of mine, "because most people don't talk openly about their own shame. He was popular after the war, mostly in Hakodate and Kushiro where he spent a couple years of his life. His popularity was probably due to the fact that he wrote about very personal things and expressed the sorrows, or melancholy, of many people."

Commercial, Legal, and Social Bonds

It was natural that most social and commercial life revolved around the *goningumi*. Landlords and shop owners frequently formed alliances based on related professions and forged bonds of confidence and trust that to this day cement trading relationships.

These groups elected officers and acted as a network of communication to pass along orders from the top. Together members would read and study the *goningumicho* (*goningumi* laws). Every family was expected to know the laws thoroughly and they were even used as textbooks in the *terakoya* (temple schools).

If there was a lawsuit against any member, then the whole group had to appear at the official town proceedings. Before the final judgment, the group would try to resolve the conflict. The motivation was strong because the whole group could be shamed by the outcome, which could even affect the business dealings and marriageability of members.

Every village kept a record of all *goningumi* members and all details about the family. Every detail concerning every aspect of life was decided by the lord, written in the book, and available for all to see. It was little use for anyone to try hiding something about his or her past—there was really no such thing as private life.

With the coming of the Meiji Era (1868–1912), the *goningumi* system did not disappear, rather it carried on in a modified form. During World War II the neighborhood group system was used to force the community to join the war effort as a group.

In an ironic twist of history, the Japanese carried the system back into China, from where it originated, as a brutal means of controlling the population in occupied territory during the war. And today, local statutes, along with commercial and social activity, still show that the system is alive and well ("Goningumi," *Nihon Rekishi Daijiten* 4 [Kawadeshoboshinsha Publisher, 1985]).

The centuries-old prying eyes of *goningumi* are ever present, ever vicious, and ever damaging. One day I asked an English-language tutor what was troubling her. She said that she just received a call from the father of one of her students.

A junior high school boy had been coming to her house twice a week for English language lessons after his school let out. "The boy's father would come directly from work and park out front until the lesson was over," she explained. "Then they'd drive home together.

"One of my neighbors saw his car out there and called the man's wife, saying that her husband was having an affair with me. The man's wife knew that there was nothing to the rumor, but the family decided that it was better to end the lessons than to run the risk of such a rumor continuing."

Whether or not the rumor was true was not nearly as significant as the impression that neighbors might hold if they heard the rumor. Ironically, by suddenly stopping the lessons, the man unwittingly lent credence to the gossip about an affair.

Prying eyes are unavoidable. One woman even commented one morning that she had to make sure the window curtains were pulled back by a certain time every morning so the neighbors did not think she was a lazy housewife who was sleeping late. Furthermore, she did not dare to go out of the house too long for shopping just in case someone would call, notice how long she was absent, and think that she was being a bad housewife.

That seemed sad to me, especially since her husband and children were gone and she was alone all day. Such a lively, bright woman, virtually imprisoned by her own fears.

Education: Perpetrating the Legacy

But the saddest legacy of *goningumi* is, of course, the educational system. Despite the diffusion of power in Japan following World War II, one can still see the supercentralized state in which it is most effective—in the Ministry of Education.

"Take any Japanese child," says reporter Keith Richburg, "ask him his age, and you can tell exactly what he is learning in school on that given day, no matter if he is in Tokyo, Kyoto, or Osaka. Japanese textbooks are rigidly defined to advance students along an accepted volume of knowledge according to a specific schedule" (Keith Richburg, "U.S. Educators Marvel at Japan's Schools," *Japan Times*, 10-26-85).

The shogun's rules concerning dress and behavior parallel those of the school rules covering every detail of dress and behavior in the schools. Young people are still commanded to wear drab, dark, precisely tailored uniforms. Those few who refuse can be subject to interminable punishment, both physical and psychological.

Many of today's youth are still terrified of being different, and they are suspicious of anyone who is. Their fears are frequently justified by the calamity that befalls those who are. It is no coincidence that the "mecca" of *kanri kyoiku* (controlled education) is Okazaki City in Aichi Prefecture, the native town of Ieyasu Tokugawa, the founder of the Tokugawa Shogunate that began the Edo Period (Tai Kawabata, "When 'Controlled Education' at Schools in Aichi Goes Awry," *Japan Times*, 4-23-86).

Surely the ghost of Tokugawa's rule, the pervasive *goningumi*, haunts every schoolyard today. As in the Edo Period, brute force and death stalk the shadows, leaving tragic reminders of a great human catastrophe.

The catastrophe is the suffocation of millions of creative, energetic, independent, self-propelled minds. And what of the cultural patterns of behavioral control that were formed over so many centuries in order to crush individuality? They still thrive.

Hitoshi Maruyama, of Kurume, Fukuoka, alarmed by the wave of suicides, bullying, and corporal punishment in the schools, saw a connection with the long history of human abuse. He is one who wonders aloud if problems seen on schoolgrounds today are symbolic of atrocities that have been seen, or will be seen, on the world's battlefields. Maruyama contends that a lack of individuality has left the Japanese without a healthy appreciation for basic human rights.

Maruyama was also convinced that an appreciation for those rights requires struggle. Such an appreciation cannot be handed to a nation on a silver platter. Said Maruyama:

In Japan, there were movements against oppressive power by ruling classes in the past. However, I wonder whether this society has a strong will to resist and remedy social injustice instead of an excessively sadistic nature and a liking for physical power.

Why do kids group together and act cruelly toward a single boy or girl? In any human society, there are physical conflicts between persons or groups. When I was a child, we had fights but not of such an inhumane nature. The fights were usually one to one or one group against another.

The reason for my question is not just the recent situations at schools. It goes back before the war. When I was in a middle school, upper classmen always used physical force on lower classmen. The secondary and higher educational institutes used to have several military drill instructors who were either sent by the Japanese Imperial Army or hired by the schools. They always abused their physical power on us for "disciplinary" purposes. They often told us that our life was valued at only "issen go rin," which was the value of a post card at the time. The military could call up any able boy above twenty-one years old by sending a post card. Thus, they were saying to us that you could be replaced easily by a card if and when you died on military duty.

It is a well-known fact that the physical abuses which were practiced on both fellow Japanese and her enemies by the Japanese military during the last war was beyond normal psychology. Mass killing in cities in China, Southeast Asia, the death march in the Philippines, biological warfare experiments on war prisoners and civilians are [but] a few [examples]. . . .

If someone insisted that those atrocities and inhumane acts committed by Japanese were due to abnormal wartime psychology, it could be accepted. But one cannot escape from the historical fact that many [Edo era] civilians who did not belong to samurai rank were often killed by samurai for no reason at all. Therefore, those acts done by the Japanese, including the military in the [more recent] past, cannot be explained by wartime abnormal psychology alone.

Under the rigid vertical social structure, power is everything. Thus, like under feudalism, individuals who do not have power to exercise have little recourse but to follow the social trend silently. . . .

When I think of these social injustices and behavioral problems, I wonder whether we are lacking some of the fundamental principles on which modern civilization has been built. What are they?

Perhaps they are human rights, individual rights, the sense of freedom, the modern philosophy of democracy and so on. We Japanese never acquired these essential principles by ourselves but were "given" them as a result of the last war. Modern society was built by many people's bloodshed in the revolutions mentioned above. We did not shed our blood for such principles in our history. As the proverb says, "easy comes, easy goes' " (Hitoshi Maruyama, "School Bullying," *Japan Times*, 1-21-86).

A Strangely Light Valuation of Their Own Lives

The individual continues to be subordinate to the group—to community, school, and corporate "familism." Indeed, sociologist Mamoru Iga, says in *The Thorn in the Chrysanthemum*, that the success of the modern economy has been achieved at a great psychological cost to the individual.

Traditional values have increased pressure to conform. Iga argues that these are the very pressures that produce anguish in the individual. And when there is no outward way to express one's feelings, aggressions will be turned inward.

And what is the helpful advice to those desperate individuals who are on the brink of self-immolation? Is the message one of self-worth and of a bright future? All too often they are told that suicide is a selfish act. Suicide is said to be bad "because it disturbs others."

Writes Rie Fujii, "To those of you who are thinking of dying, I tell you that your suicide would be nothing but a nuisance to those around you. I might sound brutal, but nothing would change even if you died. Be brave and face the bullying children as if you were dead. There should be nothing to fear, if you had already tried to abandon your life once" (Rie Fujii, "Live, Don't Die," *Asahi Evening News*, 3-22-86).

"Suicide leaves behind a real mess for many people; it is more than a nuisance. . . ." was the response of an anonymous letter in Tokyo. "Suicide is irreversable once it's done. That's it for you— but not for those around you whether they be friend or enemy."

And Mika Ikeda charged, "Anyone thinking about suicide now should forget about it immediately. The sorrow of family members left behind is immeasurably deep."

"Frankly, I cannot think of any words of condolence for those who commit suicide," stated Chikage Yonezawa. "Of course, most of them felt guilty about killing themselves. They all said 'sorry' in their suicide notes. However, they can never ease the shock and pain their deaths dealt to their families and people of their own generation with a single word, 'sorry,' written on a piece of paper" ("What the Japanese are Saying," *Daily Yomiuri*, 4-30-86).

The message of these "helpful counselors" simply reaffirms to the alienated individual that his or her life really is worthless: "My life and death are the same value. If my death is nothing more than a nuisance, then my life is surely even more so. So why continue in pain and misery?" If children are not appreciated for their uniqueness and do not see self-esteem as an integral part of growth and maturation, then, from their point of view, maybe it does not really matter what happens to them.

Such was the impulse of an eleven-year-old boy who apparently had no reserve of self-worth to hold him through a moment of despair. He had a fight with his buddy, suddenly struck his friend, then just as suddenly apologized. When his friend refused to forgive him, he instantly chose to prove the sincerity of his apology by jumping from the fourth floor of their school building. The boy lived but is permanently crippled.

Commented the editors of the *Japan Times* (2-15-86), "These children have exhibited a strangely light valuation of their own lives. . . . Not that they turned murderous. Aggression is not an outstanding element in the new attitude. On the contrary, passivity is. . . . The problem is more profound than mere bullying, and it is only indicated in those responses of attempted self-destruction. These young people lack a sense of future, much less [one of the] past. When life is so reduced, it seems to be no longer human."

The prospects for a healthy nation of individuals, under such circumstances, will not be bright unless there is a significant movement for change.

13

WHIRLWIND OF POLITICS

Your child is in danger! It's no longer someone else's problem! The schools and teachers have lost power and can no longer be depended upon!
—The Nihon Bullying Survey Center

At a meeting of the All-Japan Junior High School Principals' Association, more than a quarter of the attendees said that emergency reform measures were necessary. Some declared that the situation in the regular schools was a life-or-death matter ("Survey Reveals Teachers' Part in the Rise of Bullying," *Asahi Evening News*, 4-11-86).

With this kind of alarm going up, what has been done to turn the situation around? And if so, where will it lead? Is there any agreement? It seems that the winds of change are going every which way.

From official quarters—the Ministry of Education, long the trusted architect of the present system—sent out a call to schools to set up consultation and guidance facilities for parents and students. In dealing with rising truancy, the ministry proposed the use of juvenile psychiatrists and clinical psychologists . . . as if problems in the schools rested with mental disorders of the young instead of with the ministry itself.

The Prime Minister's Ad Hoc Council on Education Reform, pushed and cajoled by every interest group, called for a wide range of modifications and only modifications. Some of the most notable efforts were toward the fine tuning of the examination system, the introduction of more internationalization in schools, the improvement of opportunities for home schooling, and more openness to life-long education for older citizens who are normally shut out of the schools and colleges.

The National Police Agency (NPA) behaved in the usual manner of bureaucracies. It grew. The NPA decided to inaugurate the post of special advisor for "juvenile delinquency problems." And plans were laid for a sevenfold increase in the number of local juvenile problem advisors.

Those who were afraid of, or unimpressed with, official handling of violence in the schools, might have turned to unofficial sources for help, the local "bully busters." The Nihon Bullying Survey Center in Tokyo, for instance, was a new company that offered to secretly check on, and prevent, bullying for a survey fee of $150 plus expenses.

The company flyer, which seemed to reflect the fears of many Tokyo parents, boldly exclaimed, "Your child is in danger! It's no longer someone else's problem! The schools and teachers have lost power and can no longer be depended upon! ("Tokyo Police Investigating Bully-Busters-for-Hire Firm," *Asahi Evening News*, 3-11-86).

Hide-and-Seek

Conservatives believed that fostering patriotism in the schools was the kind of moral rejuvenation that could rectify the crisis. The national primary school principals' association called on the government to distribute textbooks on moral education. And the Ministry of Education has been beefing up its censorship of, and mandates for, the approved list of textbooks.

This raised outrage in China, Korea, and other Asian countries when the ministry approved texts that were sponsored by the conservative National Council to Defend Japan. The new texts' changed wording described Japanese military activity in China as an "advance" instead of "aggression." The texts also implied that the Chinese were responsible for those confrontations and eliminated the word "massacre" in describing atrocities in Nanking where at least 200,000 people were killed when the Japanese invaded ("Textbook Triggers ROK, China Protest," *Japan Times*, 6-11-86).

Recently, fifty Chinese scholars and historians attending a symposium in Beijing on the Sino-Japanese War of 1937–1945 expressed "surprise and indignation" over a Tokyo District Court ruling that the government's control over textbook inspection was legal. In an official statement the academics said, "We Chinese are reluctant to keep bringing up the bitter past, but that does not mean that we can allow the Japanese to hurt Chinese feelings by distorting history." The Chinese scholars may have also chosen this as an indirect means to express indignation about their own government's practice of censorship ("Chinese Scholars Hit Court Ruling on Textbook Revision," *Mainichi Daily News*, 10-22-89).

Sometimes the truth of history is revealed in spite of the school textbooks, leaving truth seekers to be shocked and angry. In a letter to the *Mainichi Shimbun*, Keiko Mori wrote:

A cultural festival was held on our senior high school campus the other day. One of the classes held an exhibition featuring the Nanjing massacre in China by the Japanese soldiers during the war. The scenes of the massacre were horrible, surpassing all my knowledge and imagination. I had to stop looking at the photographs of the raped and murdered women, but I couldn't stop weeping seeing the shocking facts.

Now I understand how ignorant I was about the past.

One of the reasons for my past ignorance should be blamed on school textbooks. There is no mention about the horrible acts of Japanese soldiers in our history textbooks though there is shallow and superficial mention of some events. Why has the Education Ministry been concealing the facts from us? Is it because they think we will be afflicted by the cruelties of Japanese soldiers? Even if I suffer, I want to read the true history, after which I can consider and question our past

(Keiko Mori, "Let Me Study True History," *Mainichi Daily News*, 10-29-89).

It is natural for people to want to avoid the mistakes of the past. I recall one teacher who was horrified to learn that some of her Japanese high school students did not even know that the United States and Japan had once been at war with each other. The surprised students then asked her, "Who won?"

Surely, all nations play a game of hide-and-seek with children's minds.

To Benefit Social Progress?

The Japan Federation of Publishing Workers' Union submitted a report to the Japan Teachers' Union that detailed other interferences with the drafting of textbooks. On defense issues, according to the report, the Ministry of Education insisted that a description of the growth of the Self Defense Forces include the statements "in accordance with the status and economic power of Japan in the world" and "in order to carry out its responsibility as a member of the Western world." (My editors exclaimed upon reading this, "Japan is now a Western country?") And the ministry demanded that publishers state that the Japan–U.S. security treaty was "designed to maintain the peace and safety of Japan and the Far East region."

In another textbook passage, an author wrote: "if a large-scale nuclear war should take place, a massive number of ordinary citizens would be instantly killed." The ministry ordered the comment deleted. "Such a description may cause excessive fear through mere hypothesis," explained the ministry. Another description that "the human being on earth is on the verge of extinction (by nuclear war)" was stricken out, claiming that it was an "overstatement."

The ministry was also said to have demanded that writers describe basic human rights of people from more of a governmental and societal perspective. For instance, one text originally said that the constitution "gives people the right to say whatever you think, live wherever you want, believe in whatever religion you like, receive education corresponding to your ability, and take part in politics." The ministry said that such a passage was unnecessary today "when abuse of individual rights is becoming a major social problem." The ministry also required an author to add that "people's rights are not granted for the benefit of individuals, but for the benefit of social progress" ("Government Changes to Textbooks Under Fire From Labor Unions," *Japan Times*, 7-9-87).

Spiritualism?

The Ministry of Education has taken flack from the unions for insisting that sixth graders study the life of Admiral Heihachiro Togo, the commander of the Japanese fleet that defeated the Russians in 1905. Furthermore, history classes have been ordered to teach "appropriate parts" of the eighth-century writings that expound on Emperor Jinmu, a legendary figure who is said to have been Japan's first emperor ("Education Ministry Orders Inclusion of Flag, Anthem at All School Events," *Japan Times,* 3-16-89).

In a general sense, the Ministry of Education intended to have the schools stress spirituality in order to prevent students from becoming "arrogant" about Japan's technological success. Said Takeo Nishioka, Education Minister, "We want to inculcate in our children an understanding that there is a certain something that goes beyond human wisdom." He added that this "certain something" was a power or force, but it was not the job of the ministry to define it ("Minister Urges Schools to Emphasize Spirituality," *Japan Times*, 3-11-89).

To one critic, this "power" or "force" was clearly the government's power over what is taught in schools, even when it defied human wisdom. It was this man, historian and author Saburo Ienaga, who went to the Tokyo High Court to challenge the government's constitutional authority to screen textbooks.

After twenty-four years of litigation, the court ruled that there was no violation of constitutional guarantees of freedoms in education. His books were disqualified from the approved list of books for schools, said the court, but because Ienaga was still free to publish them for the general public, the screening system did not constitute censorship ("Textbook Screening System Is Legal, Tokyo High Court Rules," *Japan Times*, 3-20-86).

While Ienaga's court action has so far been unsuccessful in challenging the authorities, other recent court activity may undermine the drive for spirituality that has emanated from the Ministry of Education. The recent Recruit Company scandal of influence peddling in government has reached into the ministry and brought down Kunio Takaishi, the former vice-minister of education.

Investigations into the Recruit payoffs revealed that Takaishi took money from Liberal Democratic Party (LDP) functionaries so that he might have funds to run for Parliament in the next general election. The web of political deals allegedly influenced his decision to call for the abandonment of social studies in the schools, favoring instead geography and history courses that were sought by hardliners in the LDP. Such revelations, and the cloud of corruption that still hangs over 160 politicians and bureaucrats, made a mockery of claims that the government was able to instruct young people about morality and spirituality ("Arrested Ex-Education Official Tied to End of Social Studies," *Japan Times*, 4-6-89).

The Sun Flag

In yet another directive, the Ministry of Education called on all public schools to raise the flag (*Hinomaru*) and play the emperor's song (*Kimigayo*) at school ceremonies. In announcing the directive, Kazuya Ishibashi, Minister of Education declared, "In this period of internationalization, we will be jeered by other countries unless we resolutely develop our national identity as Japanese" ("Unofficial National Anthem Omitted at Rites in Third of Public Schools," *Japan Times*, 11-3-89).

Neither of these have been recognized as the country's official flag and song, but both are thought to strongly symbolize the emperor system. And at least one prefectural board distributed pamphlets that praised the emperor system while encouraging the use of these symbols.

So far, compliance with these directives has been incomplete. A survey of 39,432 schools by the Ministry of Education revealed that a third of the schools were not insisting on use of the emperor's song at entrance ceremonies and graduation ceremonies, although most were raising the flag.

Schools	Kimigayo at Opening	Kimigayo at Graduation	Hinomaru at Graduation
Elementary	75.8 percent	58.8 percent	94.7 percent
Junior High	71.3 percent	68.3 percent	93.7 percent
High School	56.1 percent	54.2 percent	85.0 percent

Right-wing political groups have tried to enforce the government's mandates concerning flag-raising by storming school ceremonies in some of the districts where these nationalistic rituals were not observed. As many as 860 extreme nationalist groups with an estimated 120,000 members have been stepping up their political activities and physical violence. In 1986, Robert Whymant, a correspondent for the *Daily Yomiuri*, stated, "The latest national police agency report recorded the highest number of criminal incidents involving the right wing in any year since the war."

These extremists drive around cities in their ominous black vans, wire fencing across the windows and the rising sun painted on the sides, all the while blaring their angry message from enormous loudspeakers. One day their plan was to interrupt the speeches of a member of the Japan Socialist Party, another, to deliver threats against Genshu Hanayagi, a famous dance star and author of a best-seller who had attempted to distribute leaflets that called Emperor Hirohito a war criminal. These right-wing groups disrupted her neighborhood with loudspeakers, scrawled graffitti on the walls of her house, ransacked the premises, and threatened her life. Ms. Hanayagi claimed that her requests for police protection have been brushed aside.

While there are violent extremists on the left as well, notably Japan's notorious Red Army, the more effective opposition to right-wing nationalism in the schools has come from the teachers' unions, which have expressed fears of resurgent nationalistic militarism.

In Okinawa, where memories of the war are most bitter, seventeen students at a school for the blind walked out of the gym when the principal came into the graduation ceremonies announcing a procession led by the sun flag. The teachers surrounded him and asked him to take the flag away, but he refused.

More successful in Nara Prefecture was an angry mother who handed out leaflets asking other parents to oppose the use of the flag and song at opening ceremonies of her son's school. She grabbed the microphone on stage and, when others cut off the power, she took down the flag with assistance from two men.

To many Japanese, it was the mandatory use of such songs and flags, the symbols of state worship, that helped lead the nation to its tragic ordeal in the Pacific War. A law professor at Doshisha University, Yoshinobu Tai, commented that children faced a very severe educational program to teach them to idolize the emperor before the war. "The emperor's words were read to kids and they had to stand at attention all throughout the ceremony. These documents with the emperor's words were treated with such reverence that the students even had to bow as they passed the closet where the documents were stored. So important were these documents to the school officials that if the closet was destroyed in a fire, the principal would resign or even kill himself." It is argued that such practices have befriended neither reason nor individuality. Even today, grim hints of this blind loyalty remain.

In the summer of 1988, a police officer was grilled by the press for his refusal to help a seven-year-old child who was drowning in a river. The officer was assigned to guard duty for the Crown Prince and would not leave his station when a call rang out to help the child. The guard presumably thought his official duty was more important than saving the child. The Crown Prince later apologized for the incident, saying that he hoped his guards would, for the sake of the people, carry out their duties in a broad-minded manner.

Red Flag

Others have accused the teachers' unions and many universities of quashing individuality through the teaching of Marxism. These accusers are deeply worried over the influence that generations of Marxist teachers have had on the youth of Japan. To many Japanese, Marxism also has a dismal global record in terms of individuality and human rights.

Said one middle-aged professor at a national teachers college, "There is strong communist influence at most colleges. Some of the faculty here belong to the communist party despite a law against it. Maybe ten others are strongly influenced by them. And at some of the more prominent schools they are probably in the majority.

"These faculty are always at odds with the Ministry of Education. One time the teachers sent an angry letter to *Red Flag* magazine opposing the formation of a government committee to review the universities. The ministry responded by cutting off funds to our university.

"The teachers' union has always been very leftist, as have most of the political student groups ever since the war. But after they graduate, they are obliged to support the conservative Liberal Democratic Party because that party is favored by nearly all of the prominent companies.

"In my classes, I use some very charming illustrations from the life of Marx or articles on education by Marx and Hegel. People of my generation," said the professor, "quite often refer to Marx or Sartre in class. In our college days everybody bought books by them. It was more their view that education should stress the excellence of the lower grades and the meaninglessness of higher education, high quality teachers, national tests, materials and methodology [that are] the same throughout the country."

Officials of the teachers' unions and members do not always see
eye-to-eye on matters of school rules and corporal punishment.
The membership largely practices, or supports, the ever stricter
enforcement of regulations, whereas the leaders of the Japan
Teachers' Union have joined the Japan Federation of Bar Associations and most of the influential newspapers in pressing for
reforms and greater respect for children's rights.

The Bar Association held a convention and composed a declaration that focused specifically on the lack of protection afforded
to young people in the schools. An editorial in the *Asahi Shimbun*,
one of the nation's largest and most respected newspapers, praised
the Japan bar saying, "The declaration was a warning against the
growing trend among today's schools to demand absolute obedience on the part of children by virtually bullying them into submission. . . ."

"Children brought up in this manner," continued the editorial,
"will hardly learn to make their own decisions and act on their
initiative. They are likely to become irresponsible and apathetic
adults who can only follow orders from above and move in folds
like sheep. It is rather frightening to think that the next generation
may be filled with these types" (" 'Education' by Force," *Asahi
Shimbun*, 10-22-86).

This explained so clearly why the college students I met in the
first days of my arrival in Hakodate were so unruly. They were not
wild because of an absence of regimentation in the lower grades.
Those young people suffered thorough control all throughout their
youth, and they were experiencing their first opportunity at freedom and real decision making. If they lacked the tempered, mature
skills of wise decision making, it was hardly their own fault.

Not Content to Be Sheep

Japanese youth have not always been content to "move in folds
like sheep," as the editors of the *Asahi Shimbun* worried. While
the circumstances are many and varied, the young have always
found new ways to vent their frustrations.

"During the war," recalled Kazu Tomisawa, "young people had very poor nutrition and were much weaker than today. Food was very scarce, and sometimes we'd have nothing to eat but squash day after day. Many people didn't even have that much.

"But today's good nutrition leads to very strong physical power. Around 1970 violence in colleges was very severe. Actually, *gakusei undo* (the student movement), originated in France and it was an Ivory Tower attack on authority, often related to a renewal of the U.S./Japan military pact. But this was only an excuse. These were very radical demonstrations which involved the breaking of windows, the imprisonment of faculty, and some people even died.

"The violence seemed related to intelligence," she said, "because it would break out first in the top schools among the best students. The worst students and schools either experienced no violence or were late in following. It even worked its way down to the high school and junior high school levels."

Then there were the *boso zoku* (motorcycle gangs) that caused alarm with their circus-like stunts at all hours of the night. They were finally arrested or disbanded through police force.

In the early 1980s violence erupted again in the schools. Name-calling, breaking windows, and pulling weapons on teachers became more common as young people struck back at a system that caused them suffering. Again, such rebellion was dealt with through police force and disciplinary measures such as corporal punishment.

"As a matter of stated policy, school authorities would turn over lists of potential troublemakers to the police," wrote the editors of the *Asahi Shimbun*. "One year, some 10 percent of Japan's public middle schools requested police guards for their graduation ceremonies. PTA resolutions have given support to the practice of corporal punishment.

"The response of our juveniles has been to smooth over what can be seen from the outside, while shifting their misbehavior to more inscrutible areas. Whenever bullying results in death or injury, the typical response of parents and teachers is: 'We didn't realize, we didn't know.' "

"The Ministry of Education and the Ministry of Justice are among those now making all-out efforts to combat and eradicate the problem of *ijime*. I am sure the visible manifestations will be methodically dealt with. But by merely the inner spirit, we only seem to cure the malady. Burrowing its way even deeper out of sight, it waits to reappear in yet another form" ("Problems Visible and Invisible—Asahi Shimbun," *Asahi Evening News*, 12-6-85).

Five years after this editorial I mentioned the subject of this book to my friends in Japan and some of them commented that *ijime* (bullying) and *taibatsu* (corporal punishment) had diminished as problems in the schools today. Others disagreed. Isamu Ebitsubo, editor of the *Asahi Evening News*, indicated that conditions in the schools have not changed, but these problems have been overtaken in the headlines by other news items. And another, Kazu Tomisawa, indicated that the schools only *seem* calm now, but beneath the facade of stiffer rules and penalties, and hidden by the cosmetics of numerous committees and new departments, the suffering and rebellious tension is as great as ever.

14

THE BRIGHTER SIDE

Harmony shouldn't mean standing mute and blind while somebody big steps on you or on someone else. Harmony is only the result of trying to find solutions that are the best possible for everybody concerned. Harmony is not only silence but a pleasant combination of different notes.
— Sally Newport, Toyama

Compulsory attendance in the regular schools through the junior high level, along with a myriad of school rules, has surely contributed to the pressure cooker environment in which violence erupts. Once the students graduate from junior high, 95 percent of them continue on to high school; few drop out.

The effect of letting go of some students appears to be dramatic because the incidence of bullying in high schools drops to only one-ninth that of the junior highs. The significance of this statistic seems to have been lost on the authorities ("Bullying on the Rise, Survey Shows," *Japan Times*, 2-23-86).

Whether students remain at regular schools or drop out, they can find many positive educational alternatives in an entirely different arena. One such arena is that of the private, commercial, non-compulsory evening schools.

The Juku

These evening schools are the *juku*, nicknamed "cram schools" because they focus on preparing students for the national examinations. In addition, *juku* have become a social phenomenon for many youths and a vibrant experiment in education for teachers. Presently, parents are paying more than $5 billion a year to send their children to some 100,000 of these schools all across the country.

The Ministry of Education claims that nearly half of the nation's junior high students go to *juku* after regular school hours. Results of a survey by the Tokai Bank revealed that 70 percent of the junior high students in Tokyo, Osaka, and Nagoya attend *juku*, with their parents paying an average of $120 per month ("7 of 10 Junior High Students Attending Cram Schools: Study," *Japan Times*, 3-21-86).

The *juku* offer courses that are far more advanced than those of the public schools and, despite the extra hours of study, many students seem to prefer *juku* over regular schools. Says one boy, "To tell the truth, it's fun to attend *juku*. I meet new good friends and study under teachers who are rarely found at my school" (Keisuke Okada, " 'Entrance Exam War'—Ordeal Now, Reward Later," *Japan Times*, 4-25-86).

These private schools cater to young people of all ages—from kindergarten to college level. The Tokka Institute of Early Education, for instance, helps children from one to five years of age in preparing for kindergarten entrance examinations. When a two-year-old girl at the institute said, "I love to go to study," the mother commented that the girl even gives her a hard time when the class does not meet. (Emiko Oki, "Pre-Kindergarten Tutoring Institutions Thrive," *Japan Times*, 11-24-85).

A book titled *The Yobiko* gives a very positive description of life in the *juku* that caters to the older students—students who have failed the college entrance examinations and are still trying to get into a top university of their choice.

The twenty-five young people who edited this book say that students can enjoy freedom and a life full of activities at these institutions. Most of these editors studied at yobiko themselves, and one of the editors failed the examinations four years in a row ("New Book Highlights Cram Schools," *Japan Times*, 3-26-86).

"Why Are the *Juku* So Popular?" (4-11-86) asked the editors of the *Japan Times*. They observe that this kind of school provides a friendly and purposeful community life that stands in sharp contrast to that of the regular schools. They even assert that *kyoiku mamas* (education mothers), no longer have to push their children.

Said the editors of the *Japan Times*, "increasingly the mother doesn't have to suggest *juku*—the child himself or herself asks for it." They concluded, "To put it the baldest: Are we not witnessing the development of an education system to substitute for the public one that we pay taxes for and hear nothing of but complaints?"

Begging to Study

Students were asking to go to additional classes? This is precisely what happened to one mother I knew in Hakodate. "I was opposed to sending Toshio to *juku*, but he begged me to let him go to school like the other kids," said Mrs. Sato.

"All the students from Toshio's class at school go to *juku* in the evenings," explained Sato in a discussion about her son. "They prefer *juku* to school. My son never tells me that he doesn't want to go . . . even though he attends three times a week, two hours each time.

"The teachers are young and eager to teach because they can get a lot of money. They will talk about contemporary issues with the kids. But at the regular school, a bad teacher can't be fired because of the strong union. And there's little incentive for a bad teacher to improve. My son had seven teachers in junior high. One was his favorite, and he hates the rest.

"I thought public school was enough to go to. I believed in the teachers, but now I realize they aren't enough, especially in English because the Ministry of Education cut the English classes from four to three periods per week. Also, Toshio's *juku* has thirteen students in a class right now. There are thirty to forty students in a class at the regular schools.

"The *juku* students take sample tests like the ones they will get on the national exams, and the instructors will give them a computer printout with very clear instructions on how they did. There's nothing like that at the public school. For years the public school teachers tried to ignore the *juku*, but now they, too, send their children to *juku*.

"In addition to being more energetic and more fun, the *juku* teachers are also more versatile than public school teachers. One teacher has many subjects to teach: English and math are the two main subjects, then Japanese, chemistry, biology, and history. He or she teaches six hours per day six days a week for the same pay, or more if he or she is good. And the instructor teaches all levels: primary, junior high, and high school.

"Maybe a new teacher prefers the public school because it is easier and more secure. But at *juku* the teacher is paid according to the number of students. It's more risky. At any time a student can stop going to *juku* if he doesn't like the teacher.

"When I ask my son if he wants to stop going to *juku*, he says he doesn't want to stop because he loves his teachers. At *juku*," smiled the woman, "the teachers still hit students sometimes, but the hitting concerns their studies rather than a long list of picky rules. We're paying for it—¥12,500 ($100) a month. If we didn't like it—sayonara.

"At public schools, students are hit for breaking rules. The teachers are no fun, always serious. At *juku* they don't have many rules, and they [students] don't have to wear uniforms."

According to Taisuke Kamata, Associate Dean of the Law School at Doshisha University some of the greatest soul-searching in Japanese education occurred just following World War II. "After the war, teachers lost confidence in values," said Kamata. "So the younger students had much more freedom than now and their time at school was much more enjoyable."

Kamata knew of a Japanese governor in Manchuria who became greatly discouraged by the atrocities of the war, so he returned to a rural town in Japan to teach. "He taught me, not only English, but values," said Kamata. "This man had a very free mind about how to study and what we should do. He was a very good teacher.

"Teachers in those days had no qualifications for teaching, by Monbusho [Ministry of Education] standards, but they were real teachers for a generation of students. Now," commented Kamata, "there is specific training for teachers but they do not understand the variety of students and they have a narrow philosophy of teaching. The old Japanese system broke down and the people were very sincerely looking for what to do. What is valuable for human beings! *Taibatsu* [corporal punishment] is the result of lost confidence in education," declared Kamata.

"Of course, we were punished in those old days, too, especially by the women teachers. But now they lose reason when punishing. In the past they hit the students with love and compassion, with confidence. But now," lamented Kamata, "they tend to punish as a result of passion."

Redirected Passion

According to Akio Sugasaki, Chief of the Hakodate Reformatory, *ijime* does not exist at the *juku*. Because there are no regulations at the *juku*, said Sugasaki, the students are not imitating teachers who bully students by hitting them.

Natsuo Oshima was one of my university students who taught part-time as a *juku* teacher. He said, "Some students go only to *juku* and not to regular school at all. Regular school teachers have lost their love for [teaching] the students."

Oshima went on to explain that more students would drop out of regular schools if they could, but the schools still issue a recommendation that is valued by the next level of schools. "Since the last reported grade from high school or junior high is sent in after the second year [of each three-year sequence] students often don't care about the mark in their third year. They skip classes, go only to *juku*, and study in the evening."

One reason that young rebels may be so interested in the *juku* is because many of the *juku* teachers were rebels themselves when they were younger, observed Toshio Murata, a professor of marketing at Yokohama Commercial College. "The surveys reveal that parents and teachers regard the *juku* teachers as better than the public school teachers.

"For one thing," said Murata, "*juku* teachers are more competitive. Some of them were former leaders of radical groups in their own schools, and they became good teachers because they are so charismatic. As a result of their radicalism those leaders were denied all other jobs except those at the *juku*."

One of the "radicals" that Murata may have been speaking of was Shunsuke Nomura, who spent a total of eighteen years in prison for his right-wing activities and is now opening a private school for young misfits. In 1963 he set fire to the home of a Liberal Democractic Party leader and in 1977 he seized the Keidanren Hall, headquarters of the major business association in Japan.

Nomura declared that uniform education is not capable of helping youths develop a sense of social responsibility and strong character. He hopes to do it with "man-to-man" education.

"I am going to cry and drink with my students. I am going to teach my students what I have learned in my 'muddy' youth," said Nomura ("Former Radical Nomura Opens School in Tokyo," *Japan Times*, 12-17-85).

Learning Is a Naturally Emerging Desire

With a far less radical past, but with an equal concern for the rearing of Japan's throttled youth, is Shigeo Okuchi. Okuchi opened his house to youngsters, displaying a simple sign outside reading "Yagiri-juku."

It took a family crisis to get Okuchi to leave his job as a hardworking salaryman in a major trading company. Okuchi's oldest son, Takuo, suffered from a typical school malaise that became increasingly serious.

"The first couple of months, I dragged him out of the house by force and took him to school on a bicycle," recounted Okuchi. As the boy refused to go to school, stopped eating, and drank only water, his condition rapidly deteriorated.

One of a long string of doctors finally started to ask Takuo about school. "The doctor told me later that Takuo talked nonstop for a couple of hours about his school and how he was not able to cope with school. After the counseling session, he came home and told his mother he was hungry." Exclaimed Okuchi, " . . . I finally realized that what was wrong might not be with the kids, but with the school system."

Okuchi began to make the connection between the authoritarian system of suppression that existed in his company and that in his son's school. So, without any plans, he quit his job. For a long while he stayed home and helped his son; then he became involved with other children and the *juku* emerged.

"Learning is fun. Kids love it. People think that kids won't study unless they are forced. It's totally the opposite. Studying becomes painful because they are forced." Okuchi added, "Is the purpose of studying to get good grades or to be accepted by prestigious schools? I'd say it's not that low-level. Learning is a desire that comes forth naturally" ("Helping Kids Find the Joy of Learning," *Japan Times Weekly*, 8-1-87).

Big Business

While Okuchi provides education to the handful of students who can squeeze into his living room, there are others in the market who realize that there is a tremendous student demand among those looking for a proven, highly sophisticated advantage in the competitive race. Among these, according to Murata, is the Kumon *juku*.

"The Kumon *juku* has many franchises, even as far away as Paris," declared Murata. "The founder based the techniques on his own experience in teaching his own children. He invented special tutoring aids, and, because they aren't bound by regulations of the Ministry of Education, he improved on the textbooks.

"Also, he devised an excellent method for calculating student performance on sample tests so that the kids have an accurate idea of which university they can get into. As the *juku* goes nationwide and gets more students, the reliability of his index is greatly improved," said Murata. "It's an edge he has over the smaller *juku.*"

Another educational competitor is Gakkyusha Company, a major *juku* based in Tokyo. With 100 million yen ($770,000) in capital and the backing of Mitsubishi Trust and Banking Corporation, Tokio Marine and Fire Insurance Company, C. Ito Company, Ltd., and five other firms Gakkyusha has plans to install state-of-the-art satellite communications systems in 200 *juku* around the country. It is hoped that personal computers and facsimilies will lower the price to one-fifth the present rates, thus drawing in students who are less concerned about the personal touch ("Major Cram School Plans to Offer Televised Classes via Satellite," *Japan Times*, 6-29-86).

Other school chains have been battling the bureaucracy for headway in the education market. When one chain of schools, Yoyogi Seminar, opened its doors in north Kyushu, the Fukuoka government slammed the doors shut. The government said there were already enough preparatory schools in the area and no more would be needed. Furthermore, it claimed that big chain competition would be "excessive" and would eventually lead to monopolization.

Defendants argued that the constitution guarantees the freedom to establish private schools and that there was no provision in the law that established the proper number of schools. They contended that without competition among schools, education standards would drop and the interests of the students would be damaged.

The Fukuoka District Court ordered the prefectural government to step aside, saying that there was no provision in the law to prevent such competition. This judgment is expected to greatly increase the advance of such chain schools in the regional markets

("Chain of Schools Wins Lawsuit Against Fukuoka Government,"
Japan Times, 3-23-89).

This one decision reflects the most significant sign of the
changing times, for the court has frequently ignored the same
defense in nearly every other arena. Retail stores, taxi drivers,
shipping and freight companies, lawyers, doctors, barbers, petro-
leum distributors, rice farmers, and stock brokers have all been
rejected by the courts when they tried to break the legal strangle-
hold of well-entrenched, cartelized rivals.

The reason that competition will be permitted in the field of
education, while denied in so many other sectors, is that the
Ministry of Education has felt a loss of control, that the educational
system is increasingly dominated by unions affiliated with the
socialists and the left. Thus, the Liberal Democratic Party owes the
vested interests nothing and is willing to open the floodgates of
competition.

It is argued that this same logic was applied to the case of the
Japan National Railway (JNR) when, because of its unions and
left-wing political associations, it was cut up and sold off. Although
efficiency was achieved, this was not the underlying motive for
the breakup or else the breakup of costly monopolies would have
been accomplished in every other sector of the economy as well.
Rather, it was done primarily as a slap at political rivals on the left.

Whatever the reason, competition in such a tightly regulated
system can only benefit the parents and students by offering more
choice.

Taking Off the Pressure

While Japan has a long and respected tradition of excellent
private colleges, graduates from these institutions have often had
to take second place to those coming from the prestigious national
universities. Following civil service examinations and personal
interviews, national university graduates captured 85% of government jobs while private university graduates could only attain 13

percent in 1987. Still, this is the highest percentage in more than two decades.

The irony here is that private university graduates are getting more of the secure, high-status government jobs only because the private sector corporations are gaining in respectability and are, therefore, able to attract more of the highly qualified national university graduates ("More Private School Grads Make It to Gov't Fast Track," *Japan Times*, 7-8-87).

The government has been resistant to hiring private sector graduates, but there are indications of a loosening in this attitude. The Ministry of Education has recently asked the University and School Chartering Council to consider applications for the establishment of twenty-two new private universities in 1989 and nineteen in 1990. Also, many foreign colleges have been allowed to establish campuses in Japan and are accepting credits toward college degrees in America.

No Pressure

Long before *juku* came on the scene, private schools were offering creative approaches to education in Japan. Granted, the number of students attending these schools was small, and the government had many policies that handicapped them. Nevertheless, such schools represented avenues of nontraditional education in Japan.

A private institution with a long tradition was *Jiyu Gakuin* (Free School). *Jiyu Gakuin* was founded long before the outbreak of the war, in 1921, by an energetic Motoko Hani and her husband, Yoshihito Hani. They were the parents of the present school President, Gyo Hani.

Following the war, in the 1950s when the founders were still in charge, Americans first heard about the school through articles in *Reader's Digest*, *The Christian Science Monitor*, and *Christian Advocate*. The founders still receive a fairly steady of stream of international visitors.

Gyo Hani explained that *Jiyu Gakuin* follows the pattern of many private schools, providing an educational "escalator," which takes students in at the kindergarten level and carries them all the way through college. It is one way to avoid the intense pressure of examinations that would otherwise haunt a student throughout his or her childhood.

Located just outside of Tokyo, Jiyu Gakuin became famous as a Christian school that promoted the modernization of Japanese home life. With less than 1 percent of the Japanese population claiming to be Christian, this strongly religious school may not grow much larger than it is already. Nevertheless, it seems willing to accept people regardless of religious background.

What percent of the 500 girls and 320 boys are Christian? "We've never asked," said Hani. But they do administer a test and check on family background and the family's understanding of the philosophy of the school.

As part of its philosophy, the school administrators said that they never allow corporal punishment nor do they tolerate bullying. Partly because of the school's name, partly because of the school's western religious foundation, and partly because of the school's emphasis on nonviolence, Hani said that the authorities looked upon the school with suspicion during the war.

Today, the students frequently go to the countryside to work on their own forestry projects, prepare meals, clear and trim trees, and even build cabins. Hani also claims that the students are self-governing.

Still Watching Each Other

By this, Hani means that there are no examinations and the students may choose not to work or study, in fact they might decide only to play. In extreme cases teachers will talk to the students and warn them that they may have to leave unless there is improvement. Instead of grades, said Hani, each student gives a full report of what he or she learned throughout the year.

The promotional literature portrays a school that is a little less "free" than Hani's description. The boys and girls live, work, and study separately, and their personal lives are very closely guided throughout the day. Cleaning and maintenance chores seem closely supervised.

While students are able to select their own leaders as part of their own self-government, it seems that one of the functions of the leader is to report on the student members of his group. In a curious blending of *goningumi* and Christianity, all the students are assigned to groups of seven or eight, called "families." Their duty is to check on each other and plan activities with the teacher. Each student is expected to keep a diary.

Some evenings the students are expected to stand up in front of all the others and report about their thoughts and feelings . . . something like group confession. Boys and girls have distinct roles that are very clearly defined along conservative Christian patterns. Women are relegated to assignments in gardening, clothes making, and general home economics. Boys are expected to study the subjects that will lead to good bread-winning careers.

The major problem for private schools is financial and the Ministry of Education tries to take advantage of this vulnerability to pressure colleges into following their curricular guidelines. By offering to subsidize as much as 40 percent of faculty salaries, many colleges have acquiesced to the Ministry's demands for control. So far, *Jiyu Gakuin* has not succumbed to those temptations.

There are additional hardships facing schools that do not suit the Ministry of Education. "Up to the ninth grade," said Hani, "education is compulsory, and the government's education principles are different from our own. We, therefore, teach a certain number of hours and a certain content in the required subjects.

"The textbooks are provided free from the government, but they have to come from the approved list. However, we are free to supplement the texts from other sources. For example, we use the Ienaga supplementary history materials."

After junior high, *Jiyu Gakuin* may go its own way in teaching students, but graduates are not permitted to take government jobs because the school did not follow the directives of the Ministry of Education through the college level. "But our students still manage to do all right. Ninety percent of our faculty are alumni of our college," said Hani, himself a graduate of the college and formerly the executive editor of the *Japan Times*.

Back to Nature

Following closely in the footsteps of Hani is the *Jiyu no Mori Gakuen* (School in a Grove of Freedom), located in Saitama Prefecture. A new school, it has no religious affiliation, is much less conservative, and has yet to firmly establish itself.

Nevertheless, there is plenty of demand, with 900 applications for 240 high school openings and 600 applications for 160 junior high openings. Exclaimed one student, Katsura Shinomiya, "I didn't know studying at school could be so much fun until I started going to this school."

The school was founded in 1985 by Yutaka Endo with the purpose of allowing greater freedom and individuality for young people. Criticizing today's schools that turn out "walking encyclopedias," Endo commented, "Under the current system, students are evaluated on the basis of their examination performance. But, how can we say that a child who is slow in learning or who cannot fit into the system is a 'bad student' or 'inferior' to others?"

Endo stated, "Our goal is to create a student oriented education which aims at helping students become creative and flexible individuals."

The four-part entrance examination consists of an interview, free performance, an essay on education, and tests in two or three subjects. Said Endo, "We accepted those who were outstanding in any one of the four fields. To have diversity among students helps them to realize that every human being is unique."

"I played rock'n roll on a guitar at the examination," said Kojiro Mori. Classes are conducted through discussions instead of lectures.

Said Endo, "We teach the principal meaning of subjects and let the students think and form their own opinions by using knowledge as a tool."

As at *Jiyu Gakuen*, grading consists of written advice and self-evaluations—pointing out areas in which a student should improve his or her studies. According to biology teacher Osamu Shiose, the freedom of the students places heavy responsibility on the teachers. "We have to play a double role—an educator and someone who the student can rely on when they need help" (Emiko Oki, "Progressive School Offers Alternative Education," *Japan Times*, 4-26-86).

Going back to nature seems to be an attraction for a great many parents who want their children to avoid the horrors of the city schools. Takayasu Aoki has tried to serve those families by establishing an educational foundation that sends children to live with families and attend schools in rural villages. According to Aoki, local schools do not give the poor quality of education as is often thought. With smaller classes and one-on-one lectures, academic achievement can be better than that attained in city schools.

In addition, a boy is likely to gain in sensitivity, said Hiroko Yamaguchi of her son. "I wanted my son to grow up in the beauty of nature, feeling relieved and refreshed." (Takamitsu Goko, "Saving the Country Schools," *Asahi Evening News*, 3-13-86).

Going Abroad

Some wealthier students, like Ayako Ouchi, went abroad. When the girl reached primary school age, her mother received a notice from the local ward office stating that they would have to pay a fine for failing to register their daughter for compulsory education at the nearest school.

"By paying the fine I admitted I was wrong," said Ouchi. "But I did not believe that sending my child to a school designated by the government was the best for her education." Having the means, Ouchi sent her daughter to the Nishimachi School in Azabu and then to the Institut Le Rosay in Switzerland (Bob Horiguchi, "Top Japanese Attracted to Elite Swiss School," *Japan Times*, 5-27-87).

Many young Japanese who finish their education abroad have found that their experiences give them an edge in landing jobs when they return, according to the Japan Overseas Enterprises Association in Tokyo. In a survey of 163 returnees who got jobs in Tokyo or its suburbs, 65 percent responded that overseas experiences helped them find employment. Unfortunately, 42 percent replied that habits they developed by living abroad made them feel uncomfortable with customs at the offices in Japan ("Living Abroad Boon to Career?" *Japan Times*, 4-24-87).

In addition, there is the problem students experience upon returning with their parents from company assignments abroad. They, too, find it difficult to adapt. Responding to this problem is one school in Tokyo, Higashiyama Elementary, which has become quite well known in international circles for being able to cater to returning children. Parents are so anxious about the transition, in fact, that more than a hundred parents call from abroad every year trying to ensure a position in the school before they return.

In some cases, the government has gone full throttle into internationalization programs, even to the point of sponsoring the schools themselves. One such case is a new school that recently opened as the Tokyo Metropolitan International High School.

This school brings together 247 students of diverse cultural backgrounds with the aim of educating young people in a well-balanced international perspective. At entrance examination time this school turned out to be the most popular among all the high schools run by the city.

Comprising the student body are 192 Japanese from local schools, 20 Japanese who graduated from Japanese schools overseas, 20 Japanese from foreign schools, and 15 foreign students residing in Japan. Said the principal, Tsuneaki Otaka, "Students should have an international perspective at an early stage in their lives" ("School Aims for Global Education," *Japan Times*, 3-26-89).

Unorthodox Routes

For those who cannot pass the examinations or pay the fees, there are a number of unorthodox ways to gain a junior high diploma. Seldom talked about and little encouraged by the authorities is the qualification test. But for many young people there is a significant sense of failure and lost confidence that accompanies dropping out of school.

The Japan PTA National Council published the results of a poll that showed that 80 percent of the nation's youth did not want to go to school. Few felt they were able to do anything about it, yet there are more than 100,000 youths who finally make the break and do drop out of school every year.

Observed Keiko Okuchi, "In this country, attending school is considered to be the one-and-only choice for children. So it is a horrible thing for parents as well as children themselves when they start to refuse to attend school." As a result, Okuchi became the director of her own alternative school, the Tokyo Shule.

"Under the circumstances," continued Okuchi, "children who feel uncomfortable with, and question, regulations are considered to be problem students, and slow learners are viewed to be inferior to other students. But, I believe that a truly good education system would work without regulations and [with] a strong orientation toward academic achievement. Through the Tokyo Shule, I just wanted to prove it."

Okuchi's forty students were either bullied too much at their previous schools or they could not tolerate the trivial and rigid regulations. "Even outspoken and critical-minded children gradually lose confidence in themselves and start to think that they are worthless when they cannot get by at school," said Okuchi (Toshio Jo, "Teacher Offers School for Kids Who Won't Go to Usual Classes," *Japan Times*, 4-22-86).

Start by Dropping Out

One survey by the Ministry of Education found that 70 percent of school dropouts was content with the decision to leave school and nearly half of this group intended to pursue education in other ways. The reasons most cited for leaving school were closely related:

29 percent	difficulties adjusting to school life and rules
14 percent	desire to change course
13 percent	trouble with school authorities
8 percent	dislike of studying
7 percent	difficulties in keeping up with other students

Decisions to resume education broke down as follows:

29 percent	study at night, mostly at night schools
22 percent	go to vocational schools, technical and clerical, etc.
21 percent	return to ordinary high schools

Fully half of the dropouts expected to eventually receive some form of higher education ("Most Dropouts are Happy They Left School, But . . .," *Japan Times*, (6-24-87).

Furthermore, there seems to be a great deal of movement towards home schooling. One private nursery school owner has succeeded with a program that puts at least one foot in home schooling. Expanding on his efforts in Katsuta City, Teruo Shibuya, a professor of juvenile law at Ibaraki Christian College, is planning a home schooling network across Japan that will allow students to study at home with their parents without having to attend school ("New School Set up for Kids Who Shun Regular System," *Japan Times*, 9-2-88).

The individual most successful in popularizing the idea of home schooling has been Tsumono Isomura. Isomura has already told about the successes of his five children through the sale of thousands of copies of his books, *Miraculous Face to Face Education* and *Revolution at Home for Creating Geniuses*.

"Personality is ignored," said Isomura of the regular school system. "Teachers instruct everyone the same way, but no two people learn the same way. I want my kids to read what they like and like what they do, to learn to think deeply and for themselves."

Isomura's children arose in the morning when they wanted to and studied when and how they pleased. "Kids absorb much more if they're relaxed, not bolting up at a desk from 7:30 to 7:30," said their mother, Teruko. The whole family went shopping together, read the four daily newspapers at their home, and perused maps on the walls and more than one-hundred dictionaries on the shelves.

The result has proven astonishing, particularly to those sceptics who believed that learning could only occur within the confines of a "proper" classroom. One son is studying medicine at Tokyo University and another son and daughter are studying at Kyoto University. Both universities are considered among the toughest to enter, where departments admit only one in every twenty applicants.

As for social life, Isomura contends that young people do not have to have forty-seven classmates for most of the day to develop fulfilling lives. Indeed, while most kids rarely spend much time with their families, the Isomura children have a very close family life, supplemented by the contacts they get by hobnobbing with other children who drop by at their father's evening *juku* at the house. It seems to be a better way for young and old to get to know each other than the autocratic, impersonal manner at school that leaves a great chasm between the generations.

Full Circle

Isomura seems to have brought people back in touch with the forgotten, underlying purpose of education. Young people learn most about life by imitating their elders.

If they are raised among an older generation that reveres achievement, beauty, companionship, and justice, then young people will also learn to revere the same things while gaining the experience that helps them to stand on their own. In a free and nurturing world, they will learn to pursue their own goals while respecting the same pursuits of others.

Sadly, the educational system of today seems worlds apart from this idea. The system presumes to teach the virtues of freedom in a completely unfree environment. It presumes to teach the importance of values, decision making, and goals in an environment that is bereft of nurturing values, that discourages meaningful decisions by both parents and students and leaves goals to be determined by an often corrupt and antiquated hierarchy.

The educational system preaches nonviolence to youths within a framework of rationalized brutality. The system tells young people of the evils of bullying, all the while tormenting them with institutionalized intimidation, abuse, manipulation, and prejudice.

The educators plead with their students to learn self-discipline and to follow the rules, while those in charge display their own games and deceits in order to twist and manipulate those rules to suit their own power. The educational system claims to be laying the foundation for a wise and knowledgeable democratic society, but it does so in a manner that presses youths into molds of subservience and ignorance.

And, importantly, not one single trick of the elders was missed by the ever-watchful eyes of the youth. They saw every contradiction and every flaw. While they may not have even been fully conscious of the meaning or of the implications, these young people will imitate the behavior of their elders.

The great hope of tomorrow, it seems, is in that unruly pack of young college youths I met in Hakodate upon my arrival in Japan. They were not defeated by the system. They were defiant and escaped from class, cheated the rules, bribed the teachers, or found other ways to tell the adults what a crazy system it was. There are centuries-old autocratic controls that still remain in Japan as they do in most nations, but, to paraphrase Kazu Tomisawa, "The young still have energy!"

Every flashing signal that the youth send to the teachers is a warning of trouble ahead, an effort to communicate how confused the adults have been in trying to raise their offspring. The question is not whether the students are listening to the teachers. The real question is whether the teachers are hearing and grasping the feedback of a new generation of students.

Are the educators genuinely capable of true reform and of reshaping the principles of education or are they simply going to borrow slightly modified designs from other autocratic systems across the Pacific or from elsewhere around the globe? Will these scholars and experts continue as before, blinded by nationalistic urges to compete as great collective teams on economic and military battlefields?

A rather libertarian notion of education, applicable to all generations, whether inside or outside the classroom, is simply to follow a consistent path of respect for the rights of families and human beings in a free society, allowing them to choose where to study and whom to pay, and setting their own goals without coercion. Coercion will not bring growth and harmony. It is not ethical or humane nor in the long run, is it very practical.

Harmony is truly a virtue within any society. But genuine harmony must not be confused with the obedience or passivity that is achieved by autocratic measures.

"Harmony shouldn't mean standing mute and blind while somebody big steps on you or on someone else," observed Sally Newport of Toyama, "Harmony is only the result of trying to find solutions that are the best possible for everybody concerned. Harmony is not only silence but a pleasant combination of different notes" (Sally Newport, "School Violence," *Japan Times*, 2-22-86).

FURTHER READING

The best way to find out about Japanese schools is to visit them and to talk to students, parents, and teachers. Other excellent sources of information were the reports and special studies done by the newspapers of Japan. And for breadth of analysis, the following are recommended.

Amano, Ikuo. "Educational Crisis in Japan." In *Educational Policies in Crisis: Japanese and American Perspectives*, pp. 23–43. New York: Praeger, 1986.

Anderson, Ronald. *Education in Japan: A Century of Modern Development*. Washington, D.C.: U.S. Department of Health, Education and Welfare, Government Printing Office, 1975.

Aso, Makoto. *Education and Japan's Modernization*. Tokyo: Ministry of Foreign Affairs, 1972.

Beauchamp, Edward R. *Education in Japan: A Source Book*. New York: Garland Press, 1989.

Cogan, John J. "Should the U.S. Mimic Japanese Education? Let's Look Before We Leap." *Phi Delta Kappan* 65 (March 1984: 464–468.

Cummings, William K. et al., eds. *Educational Policies in Crisis: Japanese and American Perspectives*. New York: Praeger, 1986.

Dore, R.P. *The Diploma Disease: Education, Qualification, and Development*. London: Allen and Unwin, 1976.

Duke, Benjamin. *Lessons for America: The Japanese Schools*. New York: Praeger, 1986.

"Goningumi." *Nihon Rekishi Daijiten* 4. Tokyo: Kawadeshoboshinsha Publisher, 1985.

Hicks, Joe E. "The Situation of Asian Foreign Students in Japan: Can Japanese Universities Handle a 10-Fold Increase?" *Higher Educational Expansion in Asia*, pp. 141–153. Hiroshima: Hiroshima University, Research Institute for Higher Education, 1985.

Horio, Teruhisa. *Educational Thought and Ideology in Modern Japan: State Authority and Intellectual Freedom.* Ed. and trans. Steven Platzer. Tokyo: University of Tokyo Press, 1988.

Hurst, G. Cameron, III. "Japanese Education: Trouble in Paradise?" *Universities Field Staff International Reports* 40 (1982).

Kumagai, Fumie. "Filial Violence: A Peculiar Parent-Child Relationship in the Japanese Family Today." *Journal of Comparative Family Studies* 12, no. 3 (Summer 1981).

Murakami, Yoshio. "Bullying in the Classroom." *Japan Quarterly* 32 (October-December 1985).

Nishimura, Hidetoshi. "Educational Reform: Commissioning a Master Plan." *Japan Quarterly* 37 (January-March 1985): 18–22.

Ranbom, Sheppard. "Schooling in Japan—The Paradox in the Pattern." *Education Week*, February 27, 1985, pp. 24–27.

Rohlen, Thomas. *Japan's High Schools.* Berkeley: University of California Press, 1983.

van Wolferen, Karel. *The Enigma of Japanese Power.* New York: Alfred A. Knopf, 1989.

Viner, Aron. *The Emerging Power of Japanese Money.* Homewood, Ill.: Dow Jones-Irwin, 1988.

White, Merry I. *The Japanese Educational Challenge: A Commitment to Children.* New York: The Free Press, 1987.

INDEX

ABOUT THE AUTHOR

KEN SCHOOLLAND is director of the Master of Science program in Japanese Business Studies at Chaminade University of Honolulu. Schoolland was formerly director of the Business and Economics program at Hawaii Loa College. He spent two years teaching full time in Japan.